The Li. ,rit

Volume Four

Our Spiritual
Resources

OTHER BOOKS
by Robert R. Leichtman, M.D. & Carl Japikse

Active Meditation
Forces of the Zodiac
The Art of Living (Five Volumes)
The Life of Spirit (Five Volumes)
I Ching On Line (Four Volumes)
Celebrating Life
Working with Angels
The Way To Health
Making Prayer Work
The Act of Meditation

by Robert R. Leichtman, M.D.

The Psychic Perspective
The Inner Side of Life
The Hidden Side of Science
The Priests of God
The Dynamics of Creativity
The Destiny of America

by Carl Japikse

The Light Within Us
Exploring the Tarot
The Hour Glass
The Tao of Meow
The Enlightened Management Journal

Our Spiritual Resources

VOLUME IV
OF THE LIFE OF SPIRIT

**A COLLECTION OF ESSAYS
BY ROBERT R. LEICHTMAN, M.D.
& CARL JAPIKSE**

Illustrated by Mark Peyton & Nancy Maxwell

ARIEL PRESS
The Publishing House of Light
Atlanta, Georgia

No Royalties Are Paid on This Book

This book is made possible by a gift
to the Publications Fund of Light
by Elizabeth Salt

OUR SPIRITUAL RESOURCES
The Life of Spirit Volume IV

ISBN 0-89804-135-X

Table of Contents

Our Spiritual
Resources

Finding
Heaven on Earth

Some people look at the outer appearances of life and see only the physical plane. Others, who have cultivated an esoteric perspective, look at the same appearances and see the inner patterns, forces, and principles which gave rise to them. These people have learned to find heaven on earth, and by so doing, tap one of the greatest of all spiritual resources. The drawing on the previous page depicts the perfect inner pattern from which the outer phenomena of life emerge.

THE PERFECT PATTERN

It is easy to go to a store, buy a new television set, bring it home, plug it in, and begin using it. It is easy because we have used television sets before; they hold no great mysteries for us. But if we buy our first video cassette recorder or a satellite antenna to go with the television set, installing it is not so simple. If we just begin hooking up wires indiscriminately, without knowing what we are doing, we will likely have little success. We may even do some serious damage to our new equipment. This is true even if we have a strong faith and trust that our equipment will indeed work; having faith and trust is reasonable, but only if we install the devices correctly. So we read the owner's manual which comes with the recorder or antenna, follow its instructions, and then proceed with installing and using the equipment, until we become thoroughly familiar with its operation.

Learning to work with spiritual forces and act in harmony with universal law is infinitely more complex than installing a video cassette recorder. There is a tremendous amount of knowledge to master: knowledge about our mind, our emotions, and our body, plus their relationship with spirit. Knowledge about the role we play as an individual member of humanity. Knowledge about the structure of the universe and how it governs our life. Knowledge about the inner realms of spirit and our spiritual design for living. Knowledge about the motivating forces and purposes of life. And knowledge about the divine qualities of life and how to cultivate them in our own self-expression. Without this knowledge, we cannot hope to operate the equipment of our humanity correctly, let alone make much headway in becoming an effective agent of spirit. As a consequence, one of the most important requirements of being a spiritual person is to learn about spirit, its design, and what we are meant to do with it.

And yet, as obvious as this basic precept is, the vast majority of spiritual aspirants reject or ignore it. They scorn actual knowledge of the operation of spirit in favor of merely believing in its greatness, its omniscience, and its omnipresence. This is as absurd as believing that our satellite antenna will work even though we have no idea how to install it! Yet millions of people accept this absurdity without question. Far from trying to acquire the knowledge of spirit that they need, they simply intensify their belief and faith! As a result, they remain in relative darkness and ignorance, even though their intentions are good.

The very complexity and subtlety of spirit demands that we comprehend as much as possible about it. This does not mean that we must drop everything else and immerse ourself in seven years of esoteric study; it simply means that it is to our advantage to study the inner side of life and learn its ways as an ongoing part of our life and interest.

Unfortunately, there is no "owner's manual" to consult in our effort to study life and understand the ways of spirit—at least not in the usual sense of a clearly written guide which explains the function of our new equipment, how to install it, how to operate it, and the kinds of problems which are likely to arise. There are any number of inspired writings which can help us get started, but all too often these writings were written for people and cultures of ancient times. It can be difficult to apply their principles and precepts to the problems and challenges we face today. In any event, they are limited by the obvious fact that they describe abstract, infinite concepts in finite, concrete words— words and phrases which can easily be misinterpreted by any given reader.

These scriptures are also somewhat compromised by the mountains of books, treatises, and tracts which have been written "interpreting" them—or writings which claim to be equally inspired but are of dubious value. In some instances, the ideas presented are so confusing that the writers seem to have drawn their inspiration more from the Tower of Babel than from the spirit within them.

This is not to say, however, that there is no coherent design or guide to human and spiritual living. There *is* an owner's manual—it just cannot be found on the physical plane, written in physical words. It is an intangible guide, written in "the words which issue forth from the mouth of God." From our perspective, it would be the spiritual blueprint of the soul, the laws of universal life, and the direction to be found in the treasures of spirit and divine qualities of life. To the person who has not yet investigated these patterns of life, they may seem vague and poorly focused. But at the level of spirit, nothing is more precise and carefully worked out.

The spiritual person can learn to read this intangible "owner's manual" and translate its abstract principles into values, ideals, and patterns of behavior which enable him to master life. This is rich and exciting work, for it takes us to the very heart of our life and gives us the knowledge we need in order to act according to our design. But it does require an active, alert, and discerning mind. We cannot just accept whatever system of esoteric thought we happen to stumble across; even the best of these traditions often contain gaps and seeming contradictions. We can work within existing traditions, to be sure, but we must always keep in mind that the tradition is only a symbol or a key to the real pattern or system, which exists at the level of spirit. So we must train our mind to go beyond dogma, ritual, and theology and sense the inner principles they represent. We must also develop the discrimination which will let us clearly see the distortion and limitation which inevitably creep into all such traditions. With a discerning mind and a dedication to truth, we will be armed to penetrate the fog and obfuscation which tend to surround the study of the life of spirit.

This warning is especially important for people who already are inclined to study the esoteric dimensions of life. All too often, these people get caught up in what can be called "esoteric trivia"—an intense exploration of abstract, almost mathematical principles which are disconnected from any practical application to life. The principles are not actually disconnected from practical living, of course, but they might as well be, as far as these students are concerned. Such people can talk for hours about the nature of the rays, the composition of our subtle bodies, the true location of Shamballa, and the exact day and year the Kali Yuga will end. They know more Sanskrit than the average Hindu and have spent years poring over the secrets of the Kabalah—yet have absolutely no idea how to contact the power lying behind the words they utter or the pathways they trace in their minds. They are the *idiot savants* of the life of spirit, full of knowledge and devoid of wisdom.

It is one thing to know the Hermetic principle "as above, so below" and be able to construct a chart showing all the correspondences between the seven subplanes of the mental plane and the seven levels of physical substance, and quite another thing to be able to translate the power of mental purpose and use it to build a business or other group which successfully enriches the life of humanity and helps spirit appear on earth. "As above, so below" is one of the great principles of life, yet in the wrong hands, it is just another piece of trash on the junk pile of esoteric trivia.

Let it be understood: being able to quote the complicated procedures for installing a satellite television antenna has absolutely no value unless we happen to have an antenna to operate! Just so, being able to recite obscure esoteric facts and figures is meaningless, unless we are able to use this knowledge in practical ways in daily life. In other words, just having the owner's manual of life is not enough; we must also be involved in living. Otherwise our study will do nothing except give us an occasional headache.

To be practical, therefore, the owner's manual must do more than just give us easy answers to life's lesser questions. It must be based on a thorough understanding of life on earth, the way divine force operates, and our relation to the divine. It must reveal to us the next step forward in our evolution as an individual.

In specific, it should develop the following three premises:

1. That there is a perfect pattern for creation, not just for human beings but also for all living things, planets, and abstract divine forces. This perfect pattern infuses all of life, including our own affairs.

The great danger to spiritual students is that it is easy to succumb to simplistic assumptions, traditions, and popular dogma and accept these things, along with their limitations, as the governing force of their lives. Blind faith can be wonderful, as it demonstrates the human capacity for trust and devotion. But it can also be deadly, because it can just as easily be extended to the false as to the real, to the deceptive as to the genuine.

Indeed, faith without intelligence often traps us in an earth-bound condition, unable to escape the limitations of traditional thought—unable to interact with spirit at its own level.

To avoid these difficulties, we need a cosmology—a set of ideas or principles which reveals the structure inherent within the vastness of the cosmos. A cosmology gives us the knowledge that there is a perfect pattern from which all of life has emerged, and emboldens us to look for this pattern as we study life. Our cosmology need not be elaborate; if it is, we run the risk of becoming absorbed in esoteric trivia. Its primary function is to guide our thinking in intelligent ways, so that we are constantly reminded of the divine purpose and plan of life as we study spirit and try to apply it to our activities and pursuits.

2. That we are able to translate this perfect pattern into our own thoughts and self-expression. There are effective *techniques* for exploring divine life and applying its power to our own activities. These techniques, however, must involve something more than reading or philosophical speculation on the one hand, or faith and belief on the other. These activities can be valid starting points for the spiritual beginner, but they are not enough to sustain a full and active spiritual life. To be truly effective, a spiritual technique must be based on the spiritual design of transformation and enable us to interact directly with the multiplicity of forces, laws, and dynamics which govern the physical plane and our mundane life.

3. That the love, wisdom, and power of this perfect pattern must be tapped through legitimate spiritual sources. Unless we work with a proper source of spiritual wisdom or energy, we may well succeed only in plugging into popular concepts and theories about God, not divine life. These concepts and theories could be very helpful, but they will not contain the spiritual essence to be found in a genuine spiritual source.

One of the chief objectives of all sincere esoteric study and work should be to make direct contact with the ultimate power which lies behind all creation. This power is the source of all wisdom, strength, and love for the human race and all of life. It is therefore something greater than the contradictions and confusion of philosophies, religions, and dogma. It is the motivating force or momentum of the perfect pattern of divine design.

One of the best kept secrets of the life of spirit is that the individual spiritual person can contact these spiritual sources directly—and profit immensely from doing so. We do not need the approval of a minister or bishop to do this; we can do it on our own. Nor do we need some special boost from a guru. We simply need to learn what these spiritual sources are and what is involved in interacting with them. Then we need to practice and learn to work intelligently with them.

The exploration of these sources of spiritual power will be the theme of each of the six essays in this fourth volume of *The Life of Spirit*. Each essay will deal with one primary source and how to use it:

- The esoteric perspective of finding heaven on earth.
- The power of the microcosm—linking earth with heaven.
- The inner substance of esoteric traditions.
- The wisdom of inspired scripture—in specific, the Bible as a source of revelation about the Christ force.
- The invisible presence of angels.
- The inspired guidance of the Hierarchy.

Some of these are sources of spiritual wisdom and practice. Others are sources of power and direction. Throughout this book, the emphasis will be placed on using all of these sources to enrich our daily life, rather than exalting the particular source we are examining. Esoteric wisdom, after all, is meant to be applied, not memorized. Divine love is meant to be expressed, not adored.

This may disappoint some students of the esoteric, especially those who have what is almost a sophisticated form of contempt for the exoteric aspects of life. Such people seem to believe that any discussion of practical applications of spiritual knowledge or esoteric principles is unimportant, irrelevant. But God already knows His own nature. What He seeks is to have it revealed on earth—not by proclamation, but by demonstration, as we learn to express spiritual love, wisdom, and power in even the simplest things we do. He who knows *only* philosophy knows nothing. But he who acts with the love and wisdom of God can master the world.

Heaven is not a place removed from earth; it can be found on earth, in the midst of our ordinary activities, just as easily as in any other plane or dimension. As the Christ said, "The kingdom of heaven is at hand." We simply need to develop the eyes that can see heaven for what it is—the eyes that can see that God *is* involved in our world. *If we cannot find the evidence of divine influence in our own daily affairs and challenges, the search for God elsewhere is virtually irrelevant.* It becomes an exercise in trivia.

Regardless of the source, therefore, we must approach it always with a common purpose—to translate some measure of its light and love into practical expression in our daily life. It is not enough just to study it or fill ourself with it; we must act upon its inspiration! We must bring the esoteric into the exoteric, light into form. The word must be made flesh, through us. The moment we forget this simple fact, we run the risk of being trapped in esoterica. But if we keep it in mind, we can become a proper agent of God's life.

If all God wanted us to do was contemplate His perfect plan, after all, He would not have made us as humans. Angels, for example, are much better at contemplation than we can be. God made us humans so that we could take action here on earth. He charged us to find heaven on earth, then join in the work of revealing it to all others. If we can understand this about God, then we can understand most of what we need to know about ourself.

We can also comprehend that the proper study of God is to find God in our daily life!

CULTIVATING AN ESOTERIC PERSPECTIVE

When the average person looks at the events and conditions of his life, he does not find heaven. He finds problems, hardships, conflicts, and misunderstandings. This is not because he is lacking in talents, opportunities, friendships, or blessings. It is because the average person tends to take the favorable aspects of life for granted and magnifies that which is unpleasant and threatening. To such a person, "heaven" can only be thought of as something far away, separate from his present conditions. He cannot imagine how he could possibly find heaven on earth.

One of the ways in which the spiritual person differs from

the average person is in his growing ability to "see" the inner qualities and forces of life in the midst of outer circumstances. He cultivates an enlightened perspective—a perspective based primarily on spiritual realities, not on the ups and downs of mundane life. At the heart of this perspective is the realization that there is a vast difference between the exoteric and the esoteric aspects of life. The exoteric world is the world as we know it through our objective senses. It is a world of substance, form, visible movement, and tangible effects. But this exoteric world is only the visible tip of reality. There is an inner world of intangible forms and invisible forces which influences and animates the mundane world. To the spiritual person, the esoteric forces and influences of life are as real and as much a part of life as the wind blowing through the branches of a tree. But to the average person, they are just things of the imagination.

To most people, if something is invisible and intangible, it is unreal, irrelevant, insignificant. But the spiritual person learns to view life differently. He recognizes that thoughts and emotions are invisible and intangible, and yet they are very real and often quite important. Our motivations are likewise quite intangible, but hardly insignificant. In fact, most everything that holds us together psychologically and gives us a sense of individuality is intangible and invisible. Therefore, if we are ever to comprehend human nature, we must seek out the inner life and the origins of human thought and motivation. As long as we look only in the exoteric realms of life, we will be limited to a very superficial level of understanding. We will deal only with the husks of reality.

To study life intelligently, we need to recognize the basic duality of the exoteric and the esoteric. We need to appreciate that everything we encounter in the physical world has an inner reality. This is a simple requirement, actually. We do not have to become an otherworldly philosopher or a spaced-out mystic; we merely have to look for and begin dealing with the inner forces and patterns which lead to or influence the outer events and conditions of the objective world. Psychologists do this when they try to help their patients understand the inner causes of their fears or inhibitions. We can train ourself to do the same by learning to recognize the inner forces which condition our health, repel opportunities, advance our career, and so on.

At first, the only inner or esoteric influence we may be able to recognize will be our emotions. This is because most of us are heavily influenced by our desires and our feelings. There may be a temptation to identify a variety of warm, pleasant feelings and decide that this must be "heaven on earth." But this would be premature. As pleasant as some feelings are, they are not very esoteric. They are largely generated by our reaction to the exoteric phenomena of life.

Probing more deeply, we will then discover our thoughts and ideas. These are far more subtle than our feelings and can give us a sense of stability and strength. But even our ideas—conscious, subconscious, or unconscious—are not a genuine spiritual source. They have been generated by the personality, not by God. They are rooted in earth, not in heaven.

If we persevere in our quest, however, eventually we will pass by our feelings and pass by our thoughts and tap the inner cause of all phenomena—God. We may not come face to face with God in His entirety, but gradually we do learn to tap and respond to the divine spark within people, ideas, feelings, and even "inanimate" objects. At this point, we are able to look at the form from the perspective of the God within it, whether this form is our own personality, a friend, a nation, a principle, or a scientific discovery. This is the true esoteric perspective. It comes from finding heaven, the inner spark of divine life, on earth, the outer manifestation of this spark.

The ability to find heaven on earth is a dynamic skill requiring discernment and clear thought. There are many things on earth which do not reveal heaven, do not bespeak divine will. Such things as disasters, plagues, and wars do not reveal God at work on a global scale any more than anger, ill health, or grief indicate spirit at work on a personal scale. But humanity is able to grow as it maturely confronts disasters, plagues, and wars, just as the individual grows as he or she learns that anger and grief are counterproductive, and that ill health is a sign of a deeper problem. And this capacity to grow and implement reforms, individually or collectively, is a sign that heaven is interacting with earth.

The primary forces and intelligent patterns which vivify and inspire human life, society, and nature are divine. As these forces and patterns are translated into personality traits, physical habits, and specific acts by an individual, or into traditions, policies, and movements by nations and races, they are often distorted, diluted, and limited. Yet their divine origin is not affected by this distortion. At any time that we choose to do so, we can rediscover the inner, divine reality behind the outer imperfection. We can examine the perfect pattern from which the conditions and events of outer life have derived and, comparing the outer with the inner, clearly see what steps need to be taken to reform and rehabilitate the outer conditions of life. This is the power of the esoteric perspective on life.

Through the intelligent cultivation of this esoteric perspective, we can develop a rational basis for the study of mysticism and occultism. This is important, for an unintelligent mystic may well touch the presence of God, yet not comprehend what has been revealed by this contact. He feels the benevolence of God but is unable to translate it into meaningful help for others. If he can add knowledge and occult skill to his love for God, the mystic can then complete his capacity to serve as an agent of God. With this combination, it becomes possible not only to find God in form and heaven on earth, but also to assist in the evolution of the divine plan on earth. In a very real sense, the mystic finds not only heaven on earth, but also his own place in the divine scheme.

This kind of perspective is not the product of mere intellectual curiosity—or the lust for power. To find our place in the divine scheme, we must discover our personal spiritual design and understand, at least to a degree, how it is coordinated with the spiritual design for the whole human race, all life forms on the planet, and even the planet as a whole and the solar system. The ultimate goal is not knowledge or magical powers, but the capacity to act as an agent of God and enrich our work and life with divine qualities. It is not just to find God, but also to comprehend the God within us and find ways to give it a full, intelligent expression. Our success is measured not by how much esoterica we can cram into our memory, but by how skillfully and gracefully we translate the perfect pattern of God's design into everything we think, say, and do.

Achieving this goal is no easy task. The actual work is not hard, but there are numerous false paths and half-paths that can mislead us. And there are far more people championing the false paths than the genuine esoteric perspective. The primary ones to be alert to would include:

The realist, who simply denies the existence of the inner life. To him, there is no need for an esoteric perspective. His hidden motto is: "What you see is what you get." If God exists, He is to be found entirely in the physical plane. Since the physical plane is obviously imperfect and fickle, then God must be, too. Instead of starting with the assumption of a perfect plan, and then comparing it to our human nature and human conditions, he starts with our human nature and then projects it onto God! "Oh, yes," the realist will say, "God does love us and wants to help us, but He seems to make a lot of mistakes in the attempt. Still, we should love Him anyway, because He tries."

This perspective on divine and human life is obviously flawed, and yet it does hold an appeal for a great many people. To some, a weak and imperfect God undoubtedly seems less threatening than a perfect God. But the creator of the universe simply cannot be this petty and stupid! Common sense alone should be enough to discredit these Lilliputian notions of God the Incompetent. The imperfections of our human nature and society exist *because the work of God is not yet complete in the physical dimension and in humanity.* It is the ignorance and selfishness of men and women which preserve imperfection, not an inadequacy on the part of God.

The magical thinker sounds a different tune, but ends up doing much the same as the realist—projecting his personal vision on God. He glorifies the wish life of the personality by assuming that God wants whatever the magical thinker happens to want—in other words, God wants him to be happy, to be prosperous, and to have a fulfilling life. The magical thinker will talk about looking at life through God's eyes, but it is amazing how closely God's perspective matches his own selfishness! It is as though God's basic purpose is to treat us to Christmas parties and nice surprises three hundred and sixty five days of the year. God turns out to be a kindly old grandfather who rarely refuses us anything we want. Naturally, this type of thinking bears no resemblance to a true esoteric perspective on life. It is a pleasant fiction which has a certain amount of appeal as long as things are going well for us, but tends to crumble rather easily in times of genuine need.

God, of course, *is* benevolent and does want us to fulfill our spiritual plan. If we do, then we will be successful, healthy, and happy. But fulfillment comes from playing our part as a spiritual person—not just wishing to have all our problems disappear. As a result, God's view of what constitutes success, health, and happiness is often radically different from our personal ideas on the same subjects.

Another source of misinformation about the inner perspective comes, strangely enough, from *psychics and sensitives.* There are, of course, many fine psychics who have carefully refined their skills and use them to investigate the true phenomena of life on *all* inner levels, from the astral to the mental and beyond, into the realms of spirit. These people embark on psychic work with a mature esoteric perspective, trying to put the emotional or mental phenomena they observe into the larger context in which it exists. They look for and find heaven not just on earth, but in astral and mental phenomena as well.

But the vast majority of psychics and sensitives are not so skilled. They have developed a certain measure of talent, but usually do not understand it, and so are easily deceived by it. In most cases, they are capable only of acting psychically on the astral plane, which is the dimension most closely related to the dense physical plane. The astral plane is the plane of our emotions and our desires; it is highly colored by our personal views, fears, and hopes. The events which occur at this level are often artificial, not real, shaped only by our own subconscious, or the subconsciouses of others, living or dead. They have no more to do with divine life and God's plan than most events on the physical plane—and in many cases, a good deal less. Like the realist, however, the average psychic tends to assume that what he perceives at this level is God in action—and that the knowledge he acquires psychically is the very highest knowledge attainable.

The astral plane is just as much a part of human activity and the worlds of form as the physical plane. Much good can come from the skills of being able to tune in accurately to the events and forces of the astral plane—but part of accuracy demands the ability to put these events and forces into their larger context! Otherwise, the psychic is apt to become trapped in his own limitations, for the astral plane is a realm where illusion is supreme. The liquid nature of astral substance quickly reflects what we wish or fear.

This is advice that each spiritual aspirant needs to learn to heed, because as we tread the spiritual path, sooner or later we begin to develop some of the skills of sensitivity or psychic perception. Whether we think of ourself as a psychic, a mystic, an intuitive, or simply someone who is directed by a strong inner guidance, we must be careful not to overrate the meaning of our perceptions. We must not become a hostage to our own subconscious or personal point of view, but strive constantly to cultivate an impersonal, divine perspective. We must make an honest effort to determine what divine life is trying to accomplish in the situations, relationships, and activities of our life. In some cases, we must ask what the soul values and is trying to accomplish— and how it wants us to behave. In other cases, we must ask what the intent of God is and how it is trying to inspire a group or nation as a whole. In still other situations, it may be best to try to understand how a divine quality we are working with—such as goodwill, joy, or dignity—is seeking to influence conditions, and what we can do to best serve it.

The answer will probably not come immediately. Nonetheless, we are laying the groundwork for genuine understanding and clear thinking. We are laying the groundwork for *a revelation* through direct intuitive knowing, which we must then carefully weigh through *empirical testing*. In this way, we protect ourself from self-deception and the temptation to follow false paths.

Revelation might be considered the highest form of intuition; it is a flash of insight received by our spiritual self and then passed on to the enlightened mind. It is far removed from the visions, hunches, and gut feelings of the psychic, because it does not use any of the sensory channels of the personality, as the psychic does. And yet, even though revelation does not use the senses of the personality, a highly developed personality is required to make the process of revelation work. Only a person who is consistently dedicated to the truth and the plan of God, and is willing to respond to them, is sufficiently prepared to register a revelation. A personality which habitually misses opportunities for growth and development, by contrast, would have little capacity for becoming consciously aware of or guided by revelation.

Once we have received a revelation, we must then test it empirically. In this way, we protect ourself from coloring our highest perceptions with wishful thinking—or the distortions of mass consciousness. We also orient ourself toward translating the revelation we receive into practical applications, which increases our skills in acting as an agent of spirit.

It might be revealed to us, for example, that world peace will come only as individuals and nations learn to treat each other with goodwill—not by protesting the bomb. It is not enough to intellectually know this fact—or to realize that God is able to act more fully through loving people than fearful, angry people. We must take this esoteric perspective and test it, first in ourself and then in others. And then, once we have found that goodwill is more powerful than righteous condemnation, we must act on this knowledge, using the healing power available to us to eliminate the divisiveness which infects both nations and their citizens.

When we are ready, the soul reveals to us the nature of the inner life. But this revelation does not occur by accident. It occurs because we have made the effort to understand some aspect of life from an esoteric perspective. We have sought to find heaven on earth—we have sought to understand the perfect pattern which ought to be expressed in some particular situation. We have started with something that interested us or troubled us and have patiently worked our way from the outer to the inner, considering what others think on the subject, what inner forces are at work, what unseen influences have shaped this situation, and so on. Finally, our thinking lifts us out of our conventional ways of thinking about life, and the soul reveals to us a new way of looking at things.

This revelation produces more than just a new idea. It produces a new person—a person who can be transformed by the power, love, and wisdom of spirit. Perhaps more than anything else, the willingness to be transformed in this way is the heart of an enlightened perspective on life. At the very least, it is our personal key to finding heaven on earth.

PROVIDING THE LINK

If we want to make contact with pure divine forces, then we must seek to work with the *highest* levels we can reach—as opposed to the most powerful, most fascinating, most conventional, or most colorful. No matter what aspect of life we are contemplating or working with, we must assume that it is guided or impelled by an inner perfect pattern, and try to discern what this perfect pattern is. We must take care not to let personal prejudices, fears, theories, or theologies obscure our efforts to perceive the perfect pattern, *as it is* at its own level. Even more importantly, we must take care not to confuse impulses of our own human nature with the pure intent of divine will.

The ability to find heaven on earth is one of the most refined skills the spiritual person must learn; it requires us to understand both heaven and earth, and how they relate to each other. If we are too engrossed in the affairs of earth, we will be blind to the perfect pattern of heaven. If we are too caught up in the heavenly glory of the perfect pattern, we may be inclined to reject or at least scorn the imperfect conditions of earth. Most of the problem lies in thinking too simplistically about this ever-present duality, heaven and earth. We pit them competitively against each other, as though they were in conflict with one another, and only one can triumph. By design, however, we are meant to discover how heaven and earth can cooperate with each other, through the link we provide.

If we look at a difficult relationship, for example, and see only bitterness and disappointment, we cannot find heaven on earth. More likely, we will find hell on earth! Yet an idealist would look at the same relationship, perceive the divine potential behind the conflict, and encourage us to count our blessings. The facts would be the same, but the interpretations would be vastly different. Some people would therefore conclude that it is just a matter of subjective opinion. But it is not subjective at all. The ability to find heaven on earth, even in the most trying and threatening of conditions, is part of our spiritual legacy.

It is therefore important to understand the esoteric principles that this skill of finding heaven on earth is built upon. These principles—five in all—are derived from the way divine force moves from the inner to the outer levels of life. As we become familiar with them, they provide us with an objective foundation for our study—our effort to find heaven on earth. They also become the basis for the subsequent work of linking earth with heaven.

These five principles are:

1. **Everything is multidimensional.** We are multidimensional beings living in a multidimensional universe. Everything that is, including human beings, has its existence at multiple levels, physically, astrally, mentally, and spiritually. The inner dimensions of this essay, for example, are the quality and force of the ideas it explores, as well as the spiritual essence within these ideas.

From the perspective of the personality, the principle of multidimensionality means that nothing is ever entirely what it appears to be; there are deeper and perhaps hidden levels of meaning to everything we perceive. To deal intelligently with any aspect of life, therefore, we must examine it at each level of its existence.

We can examine it physically by observing it, studying its function, and recording its cycles of appearance.

We can explore it astrally by evaluating how it influences our moods.

We can examine it mentally by understanding its design and how it can be used constructively.

We can explore it spiritually by discerning the creative intent which caused this aspect of life to arise in the first place, and by discovering the spiritual qualities or divine forces which it embodies and seeks to express.

The average person, of course, does not operate multidimensionally; he focuses on the physical level of life, all but ignoring the inner dimensions. Even most spiritual aspirants do not deal comfortably with all levels of life; they add awareness of the astral plane to their existing interest in the physical, but they still leave out most of reality. As a result, the vast majority of people end up being too literal and concrete in their thinking—and regularly fail to comprehend what is really happening in their lives.

The literal view of life is often championed as being "real" and "objective," and therefore "genuine." Indeed, the person who makes a regular habit of exploring the inner dimensions of life is generally ridiculed as being a dreamer or a visionary. Yet nothing could be further from the truth. While we need to shun idle speculation and escapist fantasy, we must also take care not to let ignorance and smallmindedness blind us to the many dimensions of life. We must be willing to look for inner forces and meanings if we hope to be able to find heaven on earth.

The need for multidimensionality is nicely illustrated by the history of astronomy. Primitive people assumed that the change of the seasons occurred because certain nature spirits were pleased or angry with them. The sun weakened in the winter until they could coax it back with ceremonies and sacrifices. Eclipses and comets were omens of impending disaster, requiring rituals to be performed to ward off this evil.

Much later, humanity came to understand that the shift of seasons had nothing to do with human behavior, and that the sun and eclipses were not affected in any way by our ceremonies or invocations. The movement of the planets and stars, the cyclic changes of seasons, and timing of eclipses were all guided by unseen forces and influences which operated independently of mankind. This change in perspective occurred because humanity extended its knowledge about astronomy and improved its ability to investigate celestial phenomena. Instead of continuing to project our own shortcomings and limitations on the universe as a whole, we learned to explore the universe as it is, and then make intelligent deductions as to how these conditions affect us. This was a remarkable shift in perspective, freeing us from superstition and barbaric notions of animism.

The person who recognizes only the physical plane and ignores the inner dimensions of life is just as superstitious as the primitive who thought the sun could be swayed by his sacrifices. Such a person condemns himself to a life of limited understanding and experience; he makes it impossible to find heaven on earth. If he can accept the possibility of heaven at all, it will always be some place far away—not something to be found at the heart of everything he does and experiences.

In working with this principle, we must handle it like the archeologist, who finds and studies the artifacts of ancient civilizations—the weapons, pottery, armor, and household goods which are the dead husks of a once-thriving civilization—and from this evidence reconstructs elaborate and detailed pictures of the lifestyle and culture of the people who once used these things. In our case, however, we are not trying to reconstruct a dead culture; we are trying to find the inner, heavenly counterparts of the events and conditions of our own life and culture here on earth, so that we might better understand the fullness of our experience. We therefore need to view our own body and character, as well as our daily experiences, as the "husk" or form for an inner reality which is far more important than the outer expression. If we can, then we are beginning to understand that our body is a vehicle for more than just moving on the physical plane; that our emotions have a value which far transcends the capacity to feel good; and that the mind is capable of doing far more than just remembering facts and organizing ideas.

The body can be a tool for the expression of spiritual purpose.

The emotions can embody the goodwill and compassion of spirit.

The mind can be our doorway to conscious participation in the mind of God.

As we learn to work multidimensionally, we also come to realize that the emotions, mind, and spirit are not just inner counterparts of our physical existence. *They have an active life of their own at the level of their respective dimensions.* We can use the mind to make sense of life on the physical plane, in other words, but it also enjoys a rich and varied life at its own level. It is nurtured at this level and both reacts and acts in accordance with the events of this dimension of life. We must therefore learn to care for, exercise, and act responsibly at these inner levels as well as the physical. If we do not, then we are living in only one cramped corner of life.

Ultimately, the ability to work multidimensionally enables us to grasp that everything is divine in its origin and potential. It is not a case of God "up there" and we humans "down here." God is up there and down here and many places in between simultaneously; we are up there and down here and many places in between at all times as well. Moreover, these many dimensions are not just stacked on top of each other like the floors in a high-rise office building. They all occupy the same space, as differing types of force or energy. And so, to understand any one of them, we must understand them all. To work successfully with any one of them, we must work intelligently with them all.

A success on earth is meaningless unless it reveals heaven. A problem on earth is threatening only if we cannot see the divine pattern or quality which could resolve it. A relationship with another person taps only part of its potential unless we are able to relate to the presence of God within him or her. Our own self-esteem will be in constant jeopardy unless we realize that we are cut from cosmic fabric and have a purpose to fulfill. Understanding the multidimensional nature of life prepares us to discover and know the immanent nature of God.

2. We are a life within a life. It is not just enough to know that everything is multidimensional—that we can start with an element of physical life and trace it back to a spiritual origin. We must also comprehend that life itself is alive and growing, and we are part of this magnificent enterprise. If we assume that life itself is inert, then our livingness and awareness make no sense within the larger scope of life. It is a fluke, nothing more. Yet if the whole fabric of life is alive, growing, and serving a divine purpose, then our individual life makes sense. We are a vital part of a vital whole.

Classically, this is the principle of wholism. Just as the individual cells of our physical body have their life within the greater life of the whole body, so also our personal existence is like a cell in the body of mankind, which in turn is a cell within the body of God.

This is not just a philosophical nicety, but a principle that influences us every day of our life. We are not a hermit living without relationship with others; we are a part of the nation, society, and culture we live in. Even if we keep to ourself, we have still been nurtured by our parents, educated by our school system, and taught the social conventions and mores of our day. And with most people, the connection is even stronger. We are kept informed by the news media, entertained by television and the movies, and influenced by mass consciousness. Our thinking and feeling occurs within a vast fabric of social and cultural thoughts, values, and moods.

When this factor is examined psychically, it becomes clear that this collective thinking and feeling is not just the sum of the individual parts. It has a life of its own, at its own level. And this life strongly affects us. If we are below average, the influence of mass consciousness on our individual awareness is beneficial, because it lifts us up and inspires us. If we are above average, however, it tends to pull us down and coerce us to conform to popular thought.

But the life of our culture is not the end of the circuit, for it likewise exists within a larger life—the spiritual life of humanity. This is the basic "perfect pattern" created by God for human self-expression, complete with all the skills, forces, and opportunities we need to implement it. It is a living pattern, from which all human life arises.

We need to get in the habit of thinking of our life as existing within this larger life, recognizing in specific that:

• Our happiness exists within the context of the joy of the soul. Otherwise, our personal happiness will be evanescent, dependent entirely on the whim of circumstance. The joy of the soul is continuous.

• Our talent exists within the context of the treasures of spirit. They are therefore meant to be used to help humanity grow, in a cooperative spirit—not in the competitive spirit so common today.

• Our sense of fulfillment and accomplishment exist within the context of our spiritual plan. "Personal fulfillment" can be nothing more than the hedonistic indulgence of our feelings at the expense of our responsibilities. True fulfillment is based on responding to the plan of our soul.

• Our personal rights exist within the context of equal opportunity and justice for all people. If what we want is not in the best interest of everyone involved, then it is not in our best interest, either. It will simply alienate us from those with whom we are meant to cooperate.

• Our personal will exists within the context of divine purpose. We do not measure our will and self-definition by how effectively we reject others and rebel against authority; we measure it by how intelligently we respond to and fulfill divine intention.

• Our opportunities exist within the context of our spiritual design and our potential for greatness. The soul is constantly challenging us to heed its design and purpose. If we respond correctly, powerful new opportunities open up for us. Yet if we turn a deaf ear, we condemn ourself to repeating the same old cycles.

It is equally important to recognize that:

• Our sadness exists within the greater life of the our soul's ability to know and express joy. It is not caused by the joy of the soul, but it has entered into our life because we have not cultivated enough of the soul's joy. Our sadness is a warning that we are perilously low on joy. Therefore, we need to call on this inner joy and use it to heal and erase our sadness.

• Our anger exists within the larger life of our soul's ability to be compassionate. We do not become angry because of what others do to us; we become angry because we lack sufficient compassion to respond to life's inequities with the power to heal. By learning to respond to the larger life of our compassion, we can overpower the habit of being angry.

• Our failures exist within the larger life of our plan for success. We all experience moments of failure and defeat; in all too many cases, we magnify them and make a lifestyle out of them! We need to understand that no one's life is truly defined by failure; it is defined by the strengths and qualities acquired while dealing with both success and failure.

• Our sense of alienation exists within a greater life of participation in the life of God. There are times when we feel estranged or separated from our family, our nation, or God. Yet the sense of alienation itself proves that we are aware of the larger context in which we live and move. We simply need to stop withdrawing from this context, and take initiative to participate actively in it.

Understanding the principle of a life within a life, we can then readily find heaven on earth even in the most unfavorable conditions. We might have friends who have made the decision to live within the "life of their selfishness" and have hardened their hearts toward playing a helpful role in humanity. Yet we can see the limitation of their attitudes, for we know that the benevolence of the life of God is far more powerful than the selfishness of these people, and will eventually break through the coldness of their attitudes. This enables us to continue dealing with these people, in spite of their selfishness, because we recognize that their inner maturity is busy working to correct these flaws.

Because we are a life within a life, we have the potential to draw upon unlimited divine resources. We likewise have the potential to make a tremendous contribution to God's life, if we care to seize the opportunities which come to us daily. Mastering this principle is a key to being able to know the divine plan and act as its agent.

3. Life is organized hierarchically. To employ an old cliché, the tail does not wag the dog; the dog wags the tail. The lesser life does not govern the greater life; the purposes, plans, and activities of the greater life impel and activate the lesser life. Unfortunately, many people have not learned this simple truth; they want to be the one sole power and authority of their life. So they rebel against the notion of a hierarchical, divine authority. *But they are rebelling against the very design of life!*

This illusion is fed by the apparent significance of the physical plane. What happens on the physical plane is important—but not in the sense that we usually believe it to be. Ultimately, it is important only to the degree that it expresses some aspect of divine life. Everything else which might happen physically is incidental. It may have a temporary importance, but only that which embodies divine life and force will have permanent importance.

This truth is clearly expressed in the Book of John: "In the beginning was the Word; the Word was with God and the Word was God. He was with God in the beginning. Through Him all things came to be, not one thing had its being but through Him. All that came to be had life in Him and that life was the light of men, a light that shines in the dark." In these poetic words, the hierarchical structure of life is deftly stated. Above all other powers stands the creative power or Word of God. Not one thing has been created which does not derive its true authority for being from this creative power. Not one thing has been created which is not governed by a perfect pattern in the mind or plan of God.

This authority embraces the full multidimensional scope of life, from the most sublime spiritual level through the mental, emotional, and physical dimensions of our human activity. To understand any event or condition physically, we must therefore trace it back to its most sublime level of spiritual origin, or we will be unable to comprehend it. And by the same token, to act meaningfully and properly in any aspect of life, we must be inspired by and guided by only those insights and motivations which well up from the heart of our spiritual life and design. Only in this way can we act consistently with the hierarchical nature of life.

This idea can also be expressed in terms of a multiple series of cause and effect activities. The initial act of God launched a wave of creative activity which has produced cycle after cycle of change. Each change has caused an effect, which in turn becomes the cause of yet another change. This series of cause and effect pushes along the totality of the creative process much like a series of tumbling dominoes, each one pushing over the next until the last one falls. No one domino explains the reason for this sequence of activity. That can only be known by understanding the intent of the one who set the dominoes in motion.

Being able to detect the hierarchical progression and underlying authority in any set of physical, emotional, or mental circumstances is a central part of cultivating an esoteric perspective about life—a central part of finding heaven on earth. This involves more, however, than just recognizing the ancient principle, "As above, so below." There *are* correspondences between each level of creation, to be sure. But they are more than just correspondences. Each higher or more sublime dimension is actually a causal matrix for divine expression on lower or less subtle levels. If we learn to search for causes and explanations at genuine levels of spirit, therefore, we can come to understand an immense amount about the plans, purposes, and forces which govern and direct life in the spheres of our personal activity.

The capacity to think in this way is a dynamic expression of our capacity to find heaven on earth and harness its power. The average statesman or philosopher trying to comprehend the ultimate cause of international conflicts and wars, for example, usually settles on relatively superficial explanations dealing with cultural or economic differences among people. If we recognize the hierarchical nature of life, however, and have trained our mind to search for inner patterns of meaning, we will begin to see that the roots of these tensions lie not so much in cultural differences as in cultural similarities—the shared pettiness and selfishness of the human race. The problems are therefore not ones which are going to be solved by jet-set diplomacy or candlelight peace vigils. Only the effort to cultivate new measures of goodwill and altruism among the warring parties will produce any kind of permanent progress.

The same kind of insight can be gained by applying this principle to our personal life. Events frequently turn out differently than we had hoped or expected. If we are displeased with the results, it is probably an indication that we were not in harmony with the causal purposes of these events. Instead of seeking to learn what the soul would have us learn or act as the soul would have us act, we have been in tune only with our urges, our wishes, our fantasies, or our prejudices. Yet our urges, wishes, fantasies, and prejudices almost never embody the perfect pattern of the soul.

The Christ frequently warned, "A tree brings forth fruit after its own kind." By this He meant that we can expect dishonest people to behave in dishonest ways, thereby becoming entangled in the roots of their dishonesty, whereas we can expect honest people to treat us fairly, and thereby reap the reward of opportunity and friendship. If we can evaluate the level and quality which motivates a person, a group, or a nation, we can reasonably project what results they will produce. If they are motivated primarily by selfish and petty urges, we can expect selfish and petty results, even if they are couched in mighty and noble words. If they are motivated by genuine altruism, we can expect contributions which will enrich humanity. And if they are motivated by a clear understanding of the divine plan, we can expect results which will transform some aspect of society.

The person who is seeking for heaven on earth learns not to

be fooled by those who talk a good story but have no contact with divine authority. He learns to recognize the presence of divine intent and motivation—and likewise learns to recognize its absence. In its absence, there is no reason to act. But in its presence, there is every reason to act and seize the opportunity at hand.

In learning to grasp the meaning of cause and effect and the hierarchical nature of life, therefore, we come to understand the relative importance of the many facets of life.

4. Life is universal. Certain aspects of the physical plane are universal, meaning they are present anywhere we might go on the planet and can always be relied on. Oxygen is universal; so is the force of gravity. At the inner, spiritual dimensions of life, there are many universals. Goodwill is universal. Joy is universal. Justice is universal. Peace is universal. This is because divine life itself is universal. It can always be tapped, under all circumstances; it can always be relied upon.

Some people have a hard time with this concept, because they have developed strange notions about the omnipresence of God. They tend to think of God pervading life as some kind of background element, not directly involved but "hanging around," making sure we keep the faith. Yet oxygen is not a background element; it is of vital importance to our life. Gravity is not just a matter of convenience; it is integral to the workings of the planet. And the divine presence is likewise essential to all life. It is not just something which pervades the background of life; it is not "present" in our life like a fatigued college student reluctantly attending an early morning lecture! God is the source of our spiritual vitality. He is meant to be present *in, through,* and *as* everything we do, both individually and collectively. His presence in our life is meant to be significant and obvious.

Understanding the universality of God awakens us from our slumber and expands our esoteric perspective on life to include a commitment to responsible action. If God's presence is meant to be significant and obvious in everything we do, then it behooves us to start acting as though we were an agent of God's light. Yet many people do not really want to be awakened to this degree. They find it easier to believe in a God who exists only in heaven, and heaven does not have anything to do with earth. They can therefore continue to be selfish and petty in their earthly activities. Yet it should also be clear that such a God could not possibly be universal, because He is not alive or active on earth—nor in their lives.

Other people take malicious delight in insisting that God is universal, but is eternally locked in combat with an equally universal force, the Devil. This is a fiction which has an enormously long tradition, yet it is clearly just a fiction. If God is truly universal, how can there be a Devil? If God is everywhere, where can the Devil possibly be? Yet if the Devil does exist, either in hell or in our hearts, then how could God be universal? At best, He could only be semi-universal—which is pure nonsense.

There *is* evil in life—destructive, frightening, and criminal events and threats which befall both people and nations. But this evil wells up out of human ignorance and selfishness—the very human tendency to reject divine authority and pretend that we can get away with something petty or criminal "while God isn't looking." It is not a force which in any way rivals divine universality. By its very nature, evil is finite, limited, and trapped in materialism. It is defeated by calling on and expressing the divine forces of goodwill, courage, and wisdom.

The Christ told us, "I am the vine, and you are the branches." He then warned us that those branches which do not bear proper fruit will be pruned until they do. That which is evil will be cut down and destroyed until the temptation to indulge in evil is mastered, replaced by responsiveness to the perfect pattern for our spiritual expression. In this way, the Christ was clearly declaring that *all of life is embraced by the love and light of God.* Nothing is separate, nothing is left out. But if we choose to ignore the perfect pattern and engage instead in evil, then the only way God's love can reach out to us and help us is by "pruning" that which is imperfect in us.

It is sad that many people know of God's love and joy only "in reverse"—only through having been pulled back onto the straight and narrow by it after straying from their intended design. It is therefore important for the spiritual person to learn to recognize and interact with divine love and joy directly—to come to appreciate that these are the forces which nurture and support us. As the Christ said, "Not a sparrow falls but what our heavenly Father knows." God is involved in all of life, even the life of a sparrow. But He is not involved as some sterile, mindless Census Bureau collecting endless data about the number of hairs on our head or how fast they are falling out! He is involved as a caring, loving, and intelligent parent would be, giving us room to experiment and grow but constantly reminding us of the perfect pattern we are to heed. He helps us to overcome our sicknesses, mend our flaws, and grow according to our plan.

The best way for the spiritual person to come to know God in this way is by learning to work with *divine archetypes*. These are the basic qualities and patterns which have been created by the mind of God to oversee and nurture all of His tangible creation—physically, emotionally, and mentally. These archetypes are, in short, divine ideas—portions of the perfect pattern on which all creation is built. As such, they are much easier to contact than the entire universal mind of God. Divine archetypes are the ideas God has projected into the spiritual levels of creation. They are part of the "atmosphere of divine thought" which envelopes the earth.

It is important to understand, however, that divine archetypes are not just common, ordinary ideas. They have not been generated by human thinking, but by divine thinking. Each archetype is a primary pattern for the ideal expression of some aspect or quality of heaven on earth. It is fifth dimensional in nature and is, therefore, far more rich and complex than any ordinary human idea. Nor are these divine archetypes to be confused with Jungian archetypes. A Jungian archetype is the product of collective human thought or imagination. It is often a projection of the most banal elements of human experience. A divine archetype, by contrast, is a projection of spiritual intent.

Regardless of what we may be doing, there is a divine archetype which can guide us in our thoughts and actions, so that we become a true agent of light on earth. If we need greater insight, the archetype can provide it. If we need a stronger ability to nurture and support a developing project, the archetype can provide it. If we need a deeper measure of love, the archetype can supply it. This is because each divine archetype is charged with a carefully defined force of spiritual intention and wisdom.

Together with the pervasive love of God, the archetypes form the fabric of divine order and quality which is the foundation of creation. An in-depth knowledge of these defined forces and principles is therefore the basis for all true esoteric activity and work. When we are able to add such knowledge to our faith in God, then we can actually begin to participate in the work of bringing heaven to earth.

The more we learn to work directly and creatively with divine archetypes, the more we come to appreciate the meaning of the universality of life. There is much imperfection in life, but there is no circumstance or condition which is not ultimately governed by a perfect pattern. *The benevolent love and wisdom of God is therefore always at hand,* seeking to draw these imperfect conditions into its influence.

The universality of life guarantees that the role we are meant to play in life is significant. Any effort we make to reveal the presence of God within us will be nourished and supported.

5. Life is continuous. The divine elements of life are timeless and imperishable. In physical life, everything is governed by cycles of manifestation. Physical bodies grow to maturity, then begin to wear down. Eventually, they die. Businesses and nations are formed, pursue their goals, and then begin to stagnate. Fads come, fads go. Even most ideas are affected by time and perishability, losing their impact and applicability after a period of use. But divine qualities and forces do not wear out; they do not perish. Joy persists and grows, even if we happen to be joyless. Patience endures and increases, even if we lack it. Wisdom continues to implement the divine plan, even if we do not act with it.

But it is not enough just to know that divine joy, goodwill, wisdom, and peace are imperishable. We must also understand that they are *continuously involved* in the affairs of humanity and every facet of creation. God did not just generate all of creation and then forget it; He continues to nurture and support it in an ongoing, continuous fashion. The exact nature of this support may vary *in form* from cycle to cycle, but it remains constant *in principle,* just as the principles of mathematics remain constant.

This principle of continuity reveals to us yet another characteristic of the perfect pattern from which everything is created. The real significance of this perfect pattern is that it is constantly interacting with the imperfect conditions of earth, trying to purify and redeem them. The pattern is alive, both as the beginning and as the destined end of its own evolution. Christ enunciated this principle when He stated, "I am the Alpha and the Omega." Divine love and wisdom are the source and pattern for perfected life; they always have been, they are now, and they always will be. In the beginning, the alpha, the perfect pattern was the primary creative and intelligent life force issued by God as the Word. In the end, the omega, the perfect pattern will be the heaven we have created on earth. The spiritual person knows them to be one and the same.

To put this same idea in metaphor, in the beginning God is like a cosmic gardener who plants His divine seeds or archetypes in earth, so that they may grow toward their destined perfection, season after season. And in the end, having invested a portion of Himself as our innate destiny, God also is the one who harvests the rich growth from His garden.

If we recognize the divine archetypes as the creative seeds of life, we can learn to work as a gardener in much the same way, although on a smaller scale. In this regard, the esoteric perspective that life is continuous proves to be very important. To become a mature and enlightened gardener in our own life, we too must be continuously involved in nurturing and supporting our projects, relationships, and major activities. We cannot just declare our commitment to the abstract ideal of excellence, then fall back into patterns of selfishness, pettiness, and competitivness at work. We must nurture excellence in ourself and others. We cannot just declare our love for our spouse or children, then spend all our time pursuing our "personal fulfillment." We must find ways to reinvest the living vitality of our affection and benevolence on a daily basis. We cannot just state that we forgive our enemies, while we secretly go on hating them or sustaining a grudge. We must find ways to express tolerance and goodwill to these people. Nor can we just declare that we are a citizen of the world, filled with unconditional love for all people. We must become a continuous example of responsible involvement in community, state, and nation.

Understanding the principle of the continuity of life also helps us deal with the occasional unpleasant cycles of physical activity. There are times when we suffer setbacks, just as there are times when we experience rapid progress. If we know that our perfect plan is just as alive and active during the times of apparent setback as it is during the times of apparent triumph, we can work with an important measure of detachment. This principle also obviously extends to a planetary level. Natural disasters do occur, but the viability of life continues uninterrupted. A volcano, for example, may reduce everything within miles to sterile ash. But within a few short decades, the animal and plant life of the stricken area completely regenerates itself. A major war may drastically deplete the male population of a certain country. But such tragedies are usually followed by an upsurge in the birth rate—especially in the birth rate of male babies—thereby restoring proper balance.

The continuity of life enables us to work with a sense of purpose, support, and balance as we pursue our goals.

This, in fact, is one of the major characteristics of all of the five principles of the esoteric perspective—they help restore balance to our thinking. The person who looks at life without the viewpoint of the soul is confused, unbalanced in his understanding, values, and priorities. But the person who is able to look at life on earth and see the presence of divine law, purpose, and love in every facet can never be confused. He or she has tapped the essence of wisdom.

It is not possible, of course, to master these five principles of finding heaven on earth just by listing them and memorizing them. Each one of these principles demands something from us; it demands that we stop looking at life exclusively from the perspective of our personal world and start looking at it from the perspective of spirit. More importantly, it requires us to start looking at life as alive and growing, and to realize that we are meant to participate in this evolutionary development. There is only one way to do so, however. Heaven can be joined to earth in our life only if we become the link. We cannot expect God to make this connection, or even the Christ. The Christ showed us how, but now we must follow.

A CONSTANT REVELATION

As we learn to find heaven within the confines of earth, we discover something important about life. We are not designed to go through life blind to the inner glories and realities of spirit. We are meant to reveal them. But what does it mean to reveal God?

Life on earth is meant to be a constant revelation of the inner side of life. Evolution unfolds, the divine plan proceeds, moment by moment, season by season, and eon by eon. But until we cultivate the eyes to see and the mind to understand, we miss this constant revelation of divine life. We are unable to tap the most powerful spiritual resource available to us.

When life seems the same to us, moment to moment, it is largely because we are the same. We are missing the opportunity to grow. When we reverse this situation and realize the importance of growing, then suddenly life itself seems alive with growth and change as well. And if our growth is spiritual in focus, and effectively leads us into a greater rapport and partnership with the soul within us, the impact is even greater. Each experience of life becomes a revelation of the power of divine life—the power of spirit to enrich our expression of love, to nurture our talents, to strengthen our ability to achieve, and to expand our capacity to know joy.   Most humans long for heaven. What they do not realize is that heaven can be found on earth, just as it can be found in any level of divine creation. It is not up to God to reveal it to us; God has already endowed us with the talent to make this discovery. Finding heaven on earth and revealing it through our own life is our challenge, our duty. It is the duty of the spiritual person.

As Elizabeth Barrett Browning put it in her spiritual masterpiece, *Aurora Leigh:*

"There's nothing great nor small,"
Has said a poet of our day...
And truly, I reiterate, nothing's small!
No lily-muffled hum of a summer bee,

34.

But finds some coupling with the spinning stars;
No pebble at your foot, but proves a sphere;
No chaffinch, but implies the cherubim;
And (glancing at my own thin veinèd wrist)
In such a little tremor of the blood
The whole strong clamor of a vehement soul
Doth utter itself distinct. Earth's crammed with heaven
And every common bush afire with God;
But only he who sees takes off his shoes,
The rest sit round it and pluck blackberries,
And daub their natural faces unaware
More and more from the first similitude.

"Earth's crammed with heaven!" Let us therefore cleanse our faces of the blackberry stains, and strive to reveal the heaven that can be found on earth.

Linking Earth
With Heaven

We each have a spiritual self, which dwells in heaven, as well as a personality, which acts on the physical plane. These two facets of our being often move in opposite directions. Yet as the personality becomes aware of its spiritual self, and seeks to act as its agent, we link our earthly nature with our spiritual essence, producing a transformation of great significance. We discover that we are a microcosm within a much greater life, the universe, as depicted in the drawing on the preceding page.

THE WELLSPRINGS OF DIVINE LIFE

Alexander Pope advised us that the proper study of mankind is man, meaning that we can learn the most about our purpose and function on earth by studying one another and determining what we can do best. This truism can now be updated to apply to heaven as well: *the proper study of God is the way God expresses Himself on earth, through each of us and all of life.* The divine powers and laws which keep the stars in orbit and the sun shining are not easily studied by us, nor relevant to our life. But the steps involved in expressing divine goodwill to friends and enemies, healing divisions in society, or gaining knowledge of the characteristics of a plant or mineral *are* easy to study, and directly relevant.

To put this basic principle another way, the earth is a workshop of divine creation, and we are each a laborer in the shop. Through our labors, we can learn a great deal about the nature of the whole enterprise. Through the role we play, we can gain access to everything the shop has to offer. Indeed, nothing can link us with the divine sources which support creation more quickly and directly than playing our part as an inspired laborer in the divine drama. But this means that we must do more than just find heaven on earth; we must also activate the spiritual sources available to us. We must learn to act with spiritual inspiration, guidance, and love in all that we think and do, thereby *linking* earth with heaven. There are other spiritual sources we can tap, as we grow in enlightenment—the vitality of esoteric traditions, the divine inspiration of scripture, the invisible presence of angels, and the inspired guidance of saints, avatars, and the Hierarchy—but none of these will mean anything until we master the basics of linking earth with heaven in our own life.

It is important to understand that we are no longer looking for proof that God exists. We are looking instead for ways to connect ourself with divine force, thereby making us a link between earth and heaven, heaven and earth. We are looking for ways to experience directly the divine presence and work with the qualities and power of God to manifest our spiritual design for wholeness. We are viewing the emerging reality of heaven on earth as a source of spiritual power and guidance.

Some will insist that this is not necessary; that mere belief in God's loving concern for us is enough to guarantee our salvation. God will do everything for us, these people insist, if only we believe. Yet belief alone is not enough. Those who *only* believe in God, and do not add competence, understanding, skill, and direct experience of divine force to their belief, come nowhere close to tapping the full range of spiritual experience. By failing either to understand or to participate in the life of God, they miss many opportunities to enrich themselves. They have the comfort of their belief, but this is all.

It is important to know that everything on earth is connected with God—and to know *how* this connection is established and sustained, *how* it is activated, and *how* it leads to the expression of heaven on earth in daily life. It is likewise important to know what we can do to increase our access to the resources of heaven through our activities on earth. If we can add this kind of understanding to our belief in God, then we will be able to act intelligently and participate in divine life—not just be a spectator on the sidelines cheering God on, while He plays the game on our behalf.

Our search for these connections between daily life and divine sources cannot be a mere intellectual survey, however, where we tally the number of trees that express heaven and the number that do not. It is not the outer appearance we are interested in, but rather the inner life of trees in general and the force of beauty which trees reveal on the physical plane. This is a profound distinction. As Petruchio explains it in Joan Grant's masterful novel, *Life as Carola:* "Look at the rosy bronze of that poplar. Its leaves are newly unfurled, for it is spring; but soon they will be green, and then autumn will mint them for winter to swirl like smoke upon the wind. We do not regret their seasonable change, because it is the spirit of the poplar which we love; the spirit which manifests itself in the beauty that our eyes can see."

If we understand this principle, then we can find and connect ourself with the presence of God in almost any condition or circumstance of life. We can link ourself with divine goodwill just as much by learning to forgive the hostility of an enemy, for example, as we can by comforting a friend with compassion. In each case, we go beyond the outer appearance and tap the inner life of goodwill and its innate pattern of perfection. From this, we then discover what form of expression is best for conveying the essence of this spiritual life into manifestation, for linking earth with heaven.

As always, there will be those who will condemn this proposition as almost blasphemous, such as those who habitually think of heaven as a realm far removed from earth. These people also make the assumption that God remains outside His creation, unsullied by involvement in human life, except to criticize. Yet these assumptions constitute two of the most serious stumbling blocks to effective esoteric study and work. God *is* involved in our world, and we are meant to be involved in His life by making the effort to express heaven on earth. We begin by finding heaven on earth, then acting on this revelation—in other words, linking earth with heaven. This is what we are summoned to demonstrate, each in our own way.

This demonstration needs to occur within us. It is one thing to understand that a poplar tree expresses its divine spirit season after season, and quite another to translate this understanding into something which lets us contact the presence of God in our own thoughts, attitudes, and activities. Yet it only makes sense that God is closest to us in our own inner nature and daily self-expression. He may use the poplar to remind us of the beauty within our own nature, but we cannot substitute the inner quality of the poplar for our own inner connections. If we cannot find God within ourself and tap our own inner sources of divine strength, love, and wisdom, we may risk not finding God at all. And there is good reason to emphasize this risk. As Paul said many years ago, the things of the spirit must be known in spirit—that is, in the consciousness of spiritual insight and love. A genuine, heartfelt knowledge of God can only begin within ourself, as we extend our consciousness so that we are able to add to our awareness and insight, not just accumulate more facts and theories. By stretching our capacity to be aware, we tap an infinite source of divine love, wisdom, and strength within ourself. And as we find and demonstrate this divinity within ourself, we then acquire the "eyes to see" the presence of God elsewhere.

Being limited in our awareness and experience is a great handicap which is too readily overlooked by all too many people. Not having an awareness or appreciation of the subtleties of the life of spirit, these people scorn the notion that there is anything beyond *their* understanding. But such blindness destroys our capacity to grow and learn.

Despite the obvious truth of this principle, humanity is full of joyless people who insist on projecting their emptiness on the whole canvas of human life. Finding no joy within themselves, they conclude that life is joyless and view the joy of others as mere silliness. What they have failed to do is expand their awareness beyond their personal joylessness, so that they could discover their own heritage of divine joy.

Let it be clearly understood: a person who is full of bitterness and ugliness will fail to see the beauty and gentleness of life, just as a person who is unable to accept anything beyond traditional ideas and tangible facts will fail to see the invisible presence of God—*until he works to expand his awareness and thinking!*

Fortunately, the work of expanding our awareness and insight so that we find and contact heaven on earth is not nearly as difficult as most people imagine. It is based on common sense and practicality—not on some imaginary leap of fantasy or faith. The ancients often referred to each individual as a microcosm who reflects the macrocosm of universal life, just as a single drop of dew on the branch of a tree may reflect a whole landscape, if correctly viewed. To them, of course, our individuality included more than just our body and personality; it also included our spiritual self. This, together with the body and the personality, formed a true microcosm of divine life—a spiritual being acting through our thoughts, feelings, and activities. By expanding our awareness to include this perspective, we are able to discover the universal within the individual, the ineffable within the knowable, and the intangible within the tangible.

This is something more than philosophical speculation or otherworldly meditation. It is a practical lesson of learning how

God works—through us, through others, and through all of life. To bring an old cliché back to life, it is the process of leading a horse to water *and* teaching it how to drink. God may be able to work through us even if we do not acquire this skill, but as we learn to link the elements of our earthly life with their proper divine sources, we greatly expand our usefulness as a laborer in the workshop of divine creation.

Unquestionably, some people will remain satisfied with traditional religious and philosophical practices. For the most part, these are the people who characterize the work of spirit more as salvation than creation. Salvation certainly is an important facet of the work of spirit on earth, but it does not embrace the full work and activity. As salvation occurs, it is meant to lead to creation and responsible involvement in life. We are meant to add knowledge and skill to our faith and obedience, so that God can make better use of us. If we truly want to cooperate with God's design for us, we must begin acting from the perspective of this design, and this requires wisdom as well as belief! If we truly want to partake of the inner wealth of the divine treasures of life, we must learn to tap our inner sources of wisdom, love, and talent, and express these forces constructively in our own life.

Humanity, with all its intelligence, skill, and potential for creative thought, nurturing feeling, and productive activity, is indeed a proper physical symbol for the creative life and expression of God. Individually, we may have a lot to learn before we fulfill our promise as a microcosm within the macrocosm of God's wholeness—but the promise already exists, as our birthright. And if we can learn to think of ourself in this way, we acquire an important key to comprehending the nature of God as well as the power of God within us. It is in the collective lives of humanity, more poignantly than anywhere else on earth, that the symbolic and the real are joined as the form and life of God. The more we understand how the real life of God vivifies the form of our mind, emotions, and body, the more we can express this divine life and wholeness at all times, and be true to its design.

The challenge to each of us individually, therefore, is to locate and cultivate the wellsprings of divine life *within ourself* which are meant to serve as our primary sources of divine strength and inspiration. There are three of these sources—divine light, love, and will. Each is as important as the other, and each must be properly linked with our existing talents, values, attitudes, and activities.

1. We must learn to link our thoughts and concepts with the light of divine life, producing creative inspiration and clear understanding.

2. We must learn to link our emotions and feelings with divine love, producing a mature capacity to nurture life on the physical plane in harmony with divine design.

3. We must learn to link our acts and behavior with divine will, producing an enlightened ability to translate abstract plans into physical realities.

To be successful in this endeavor, however, we must be sure to proceed with balance. We need to do more than feel God's love for us—we must be able to express this love to others through our feelings and actions. We need to do more than believe that God understands our needs and will guide us—we should be able to comprehend what we are designed to do and know how to perform in this manner. We need to do more than accept the fact of divine will—we should demonstrate the power of divine will in our approach to life. Above all, we need to do more than just touch the presence of God in our midst—we should be able to reveal God in everything we do. Finding and tapping the wellspring of divine life within us means much more than just being inspired by good ideas and bathed in good feelings. It is a process of growth of the whole stature of our being toward the divine perfection designed for us.

For this reason, it is important to approach this search for the wellspring of divine life with a proper esoteric perspective, as outlined in the preceding essay. An esoteric perspective will prevent us from personalizing our search with preconceived prejudices and expectations; it will protect us from substituting our own plan or design for the divine plan.

As described in the last essay, there are five basic principles on which a proper esoteric perspective must be based:

1. Life is multidimensional.

2. Life exists within a greater life.

3. Life is organized hierarchically.
4. Life is universal.
5. Life is continuous.

In this essay, we will use these five principles to organize our effort to locate and tap the three primary sources of divine life within us—the wellsprings of light, love, and will. In this way, we will be guided to a more accurate understanding of each of these three great streams of divine life—and the ways they are meant to be revealed through our own life.

Ultimately, the search for God is always a search for our true purpose as a spiritual being, united with God and capable of acting as an agent of divine light, love, and will.

STANDING IN THE LIGHT

Scripture tells us that the light of the world, the Christ, can illuminate our individual awareness as well as the world as a whole. This light is available to everyone who seeks it, but it comes from just one source, the mind of God. It comes to each of us from within, through the link we have built with divine intelligence, bringing us guidance, inspiration, and enlightenment especially tailored to our needs and requirements. It may come as a moment of revelation, a flash of insight, an inner knowing, or a gradual comprehension of what we need to be or do. But it wells up within us as a recognition of the light of our inner wisdom.

The nature of this illumination has been described by many great teachers and inspired writers, but we cannot acquire the light by reading about it, any more than we can smell the perfume and sense the full radiant beauty of a flower by reading a botany text. We need direct experience of this light, if we are to be illuminated. We must train the mind to seek out, find, and tap the mind of God—the source of light within us. This will require something more than intellectual study.

Yet this is not to imply that intellectual study does not play a role in the illumination of the mind—or in any way interferes with it. The mind must be well trained to register and process the light it receives—to "stand in the light"—and this requires a strong

and well-disciplined intellect. Still, as obvious as this requirement is, there are nonetheless thousands of people who believe
that the intellect is the appendix of the spiritual life, a useless
organ that can do nothing but cause trouble. These people try
to "kill" the mind, usually by adopting a meditative technique
which requires them to imitate the life of a rock. What they overlook is that mental and emotional deadness prepares us only for
emptiness and stupidity—not for illumination, compassion, and
creativity!

To receive illumination, we must have an inquiring mind
which is alert, prepared, and ready to respond to inspiration and
intuition. It cannot be lazy and indifferent; it must be alert,
interested in the many aspects of our life, and constantly seeking
to cultivate a true esoteric perspective—both in and out of
meditation. We can prepare the mind in this way by studying
philosophical and esoteric literature, but we must do more than
this alone. We must teach the mind to rise up to its highest
capacity and understanding, then stretch beyond it, always
trying to become a better agent of light. Above all, we must
engage the mind in a constant investigation of the meaning and
purpose of the phenomena of life in and all around us.

This investigation will teach us that the mind does much,
much more than process facts and opinions; at its highest level,
it can reveal to us the divine blueprints and laws which govern
all life. As we learn to apply these blueprints and laws to our own
life, the light of the mind of God illuminates our thinking and
understanding. Standing in this light, we are then able to
discover our spiritual design and how it is coordinated with the
spiritual design of the whole human race and all other life forms
on the planet—even the design for this planet and solar system.
Only then can we begin to comprehend the wonders and glory
that God has prepared for each of us; only then can we grasp the
creative powers available to us by tapping the treasures of the
kingdom of God within us.

Ultimately, our goal is not knowledge or magical power, but
the capacity to assume our full spiritual role as an *agent* of God
and use these divine powers in our individual life. Our goal is not
just to find God (Who is not lost in any event), but to *comprehend*
the nature of God within us and give His divine life a full and

intelligent expression in our own life. This is what it means to stand in the light.

The bridge that links us with this light and allows us to express it is built through our own intelligent effort and experience. Once the bridge is built, it connects us with a constant source of light—the light of the archetypal patterns of the mind of God. This inaugurates a whole new level of thinking which might more accurately be called *realization* than *thinking*.

The average person "thinks" by brooding over or reflecting on a collection of facts or opinions. This activity seldom brings heaven to earth. More typically, it plugs us into our wish life, our prejudices, our hopes, and our fears. Yet human thinking *can* be plugged into the archetypal patterns of the mind of God. Then, as need arises in daily life, the thoughts and inspirations which flood our awareness reveal to us what is real and what is not. They illuminate the mind so that we can see clearly and precisely what needs to be done, and how to do it. They point the way toward creating heaven on earth—whether our attention happens to be focused on creating a new taste sensation in the kitchen or solving some complex management problem at work.

Understanding this, it is now possible to describe the source of divine light within us in finer detail by examining it in terms of the five principles of the esoteric perspective. In this way, we can penetrate to the essence of what it means to "stand in the light."

The light of the mind is multidimensional. Thinking multidimensionally means that we have the capacity to move comfortably between the concrete world and the realm of abstract and symbolic thought. The capacity to think multidimensionally allows us to speculate successfully on the meaning of events (drawing conclusions from a mass of data), work creatively (moving from abstractions and symbols to specific acts and forms), and entertain abstract and intangible forces (moving from concrete needs to philosophical insights). We are able to be aware of the source of our inspiration, the plans it leads to, and the physical application of these ideas, all at the same time.

The engineer thinks multidimensionally when he or she translates a general concept of a complex design problem into specific details of finite blueprints and specifications. A novelist does it when he or she generates a complex plot, then breathes life into it through detailed characterizations and dialogue. Ordinary people think multidimensionally when they reflect on the meaning of the events of their day and begin to move from the details of the experience to their broader implications and relevance.

The spiritual value of thinking multidimensionally is that it enables us to remain attuned to the true spiritual source of our thinking even while working out the most mundane details. It makes spiritual thinking a practical proposition, giving us the ability to discern the different components of ideas we are working with—their spiritual origins, their creative potential, our emotional reactions to them, and their physical applications. In this way, we can move comfortably between the concrete and the abstract, knowing always what is of heaven, what is of earth, and how they both can best be harnessed.

A good example of the relevance of multidimensionality to our thinking would be the issue of self-esteem. Most of us build our self-concept and self-esteem on the foundation of our successes and failures in life *as judged from the perspective of our personal feelings and expectations.* But there are several levels or dimensions to these successes and failures. There are the actual physical experiences and the sequence in which they happened. In addition, there are also our emotional reactions and our perception of what others think about us. Added to these reactions are concepts of self-esteem acquired from our parents, church, and peers, which strongly color how we actually feel about ourself. All of these dimensions are involved in generating our self-esteem, yet if we stop here, we will not link earth with heaven.

In addition to these levels, we must also consider the intent and design of spirit for our life. This is the source of "heaven on earth" for our self-esteem. If we attempt to see ourself and our behavior in this light, we may find that our "failure" to please our peers is unimportant—whereas our "success" in personal popularity, from an esoteric perspective, is only an index of our charm, not a measure of our usefulness or achievements on earth. We may find that our "failure" to resolve a conflict with a family member is not nearly as important as our "successful" effort to be patient, understanding, and helpful with this person.

By attempting to weigh our experiences in the light of our spiritual self, we can glimpse the true value of what we have accomplished, while also putting our emotional reactions in a healthy and disciplined perspective. If we examine ourself from all dimensions of our being, including the spiritual level, we can reveal heaven in us through the way we think about ourself. We tap the inner light.

Our life exists within a greater life. This principle often has a dramatic impact on opening up new light. A person who is puzzled by changes at work, for example, can use the principle of a life within a life to see that he has been looking at these changes only from his own highly personalized wants and wishes, while his boss has another view, and the company as a whole has yet a third. To cooperate effectively with the changes being made, he must see himself not as an "exploited" employee, but as a part of the larger endeavor of his company, its management team, the entire industry in which he works, and the market it serves. Only then will it be possible to identify with and understand the real meaning of the changes which have occurred in corporate policy.

On a more personal level, many of us are inclined to blame others, or the most recent events of our life, for our recurring problems. But this is a highly superficial view of events. The seed of most personal problems lies mainly in the flaws and weaknesses of our own character and makeup. We therefore need to examine what we have done, or failed to do, which led to this sequence of hardship. Even more importantly, we need to examine what habit of character causes us to commit this mistake *repeatedly*. If we will do this, we will see that our behavior and reactions draw life from our personal values, convictions, moods, and approach to life. In other words, the real "life" of the problem is fed by the greater life of our personal immaturity.

Fortunately, this same principle also teaches us that if our problems can feed on the larger life of our immaturity, we can likewise learn to draw strength from the greater life of our spiritual stature and use this strength to heal these problems—permanently. We are never meant to cower in the light, but to stand in it. The revelation that our life exists within a larger life is meant to give us the strength to contact whatever spiritual resources we need to redirect our thinking, habits, attitudes, and behavior, thereby reforming our character as well as expressing a new and more positive side of our humanity.

The universality of life. The mere appearance of universality does not always reveal the light of divine life. Social activists and muckrakers would have us believe that crime, poverty, and corruption are virtually universal in society. Many good people surveying the life around them, conclude that suffering and grief are universal aspects of human life. Yet all of these people are making a simplistic mistake. While crime, hunger, and pain are common place, they are certainly not universal, all pervasive.

On the other hand, our capacity to share in the life of humanity, through the medium of our emotions or our thoughts, *is* universal, all-pervasive. If we choose to attune our feelings only to pain and grief, we may mistakenly conclude that these conditions are universal. We forget that we also share many common elements of happiness, culture, experience, heritage, and knowledge.

The spiritual person understands, however, that we all share much more than these commonplace elements of human life. We share divine beauty, grace, wisdom, goodwill, strength, joy, and peace—indeed, all the treasures of the kingdom, all the fruits of spirit, as well as the omnipresent love of God. As we strive to add the inspiration of these treasures to our thinking, and develop practical skills and talents in expressing them, we become more universal in our outlook.

The ultimate value of the principle of universality is that it helps us enter into oneness—the oneness that we can find only in our union with God and fellowship with one another on a spiritual wavelength. As a result, we are able to think and act with a sense of completeness. Instead of dwelling on the imperfection and flaws of life, we consistently link ourself with the source of oneness within us and apply its perfect design and blueprint to healing that which is imperfect.

A good example of this principle at work is a very common form of illusion. We think that we alone have a particular problem. Or we believe that we must somehow face our problems with very limited resources and almost no hope for success. When such is the case, we need to stand in the light and reconnect with our spiritual heritage. We need to remember that the benevolent wisdom and love of God is present in each of us—and in all of our problems and opportunities as well. Each of our problems is a call to us to summon an effective solution. Each of our opportunities is a summons to us to call forth our capacity to act.

The principle of universality also helps us comprehend that each of us is important, and everything we do is significant, for we carry the presence of God in the innermost reaches of our heart and mind. As we learn to stand in the light of this universality, we come to understand the promise in scripture: "Eye has not seen and ear has not heard, nor has it entered into the minds of men the glory that God has prepared for us."

The continuity of life. The principle of continuity introduces us to and teaches us the meaning of accountability. Because life is continuous from moment to moment, we have the capacity to recognize the outcome of our actions—and therefore the responsibility to do so. For a long time, we busy the mind with finding rationalizations for our lack of responsibility. But as we strive to stand in the light, the value of accountability grows in our awareness. We become aware of recurring patterns of thought and feeling, and their usual consequences. Based on this, we are able to see what changes need to be made to improve our life.

The continuity of life teaches us that we live in an orderly universe governed by law. These laws are not elusive or unknown; they are easily known. The laws of right human relationships, for instance, can be discerned by examining the type of behavior which stabilizes a relationship and helps it endure—and by contrasting it with the kind of behavior which undermines relationships and causes them to fail. This is not a matter of divine decree, just a matter of illumined common sense. Yet we draw this sensibility from an understanding of divine designs and patterns.

When humanity tries to deviate from its destined plan, it is divine law which brings us back. Ideally, we will be sufficiently attuned to these laws that the correction will occur entirely at inner levels. But in less responsive people, who are unable to stand firmly in the light, the force of divine law may have to color the events of their lives and the way friends respond. Still, the principle remains active and effective. The only difference is the level of our conscious cooperation with it—the degree to which we *reveal* the light of heaven on earth through our actions.

For the spiritual aspirant, the continuity of life has a special meaning. Because of this principle, he is able to understand that the soul continues to recognize the unfinished business and unresolved conflicts to be healed, no matter how much the personality persists in ignoring them or rationalizing them. The light of divine life guides his conscience and sense of direction, so that he can accept these elements of his life and work more closely with the plan of spirit for him.

The ultimate value of continuity in the thinking of spiritual people is that it enables us to cultivate a structure of stable divine qualities which strengthens our thinking while it aligns us to the plan of God. We discover the secret of continuity, which is a strong foundation of values and convictions on which we can act. The light of continuity reveals the meaning of our commitments, even while it connects us with the persistence we need to fulfill them. So often, human misery is a direct or indirect consequence of the failure to recognize and respond to responsibilities and good opportunities. Much misfortune could be avoided if we would integrate the principle of continuity more fully into our thinking.

God supports and rewards those who abide by His commandments. Yet these commandments are not in any way the rules and regulations of a tyrant; they are the living streams of divine light which comprise one of our greatest sources of spiritual understanding. If we can understand this simple idea, we should be able to appreciate how the universe will support right thinking and action in our life.

Life is hierarchical. The light of the mind of God does more than just reveal reality. It also impels us to think hierarchically and begin to rank priorities and values in terms of spiritual importance. The average person tends to order his priorities and values in terms of what is most remunerative or popular—or least troublesome. But as the spiritual person learns to stand in the light, his thinking becomes more and more influenced by hierarchical concerns. He begins to make decisions based on what spirit selects as most important and valuable—not just what the emotions like, or friends approve, or the expediency of the moment. In this way, he builds a structure of thinking which adds meaning and value to his activities. Decisions that the average person would regard as a tremendous burden or sacrifice are seen by such an individual as a noble contribution to the life of spirit.

The practical application of this principle is that it helps us set realistic priorities so that we can allocate time and effort where it will be most productive for us and those we serve. Yet the real power of this principle is that it helps us understand the law of cause and effect as it operates in our life. The average person blames his parents, society, circumstances, or just bad luck for his problems. Yet we rarely are blameless for our problems and hardships. Almost everything that happens to us today can be traced back to seeds we have sown in the past, as we have mistreated others, neglected responsibilities, and so on. When events seem to occur without any obvious antecedent, it is usually just a sign that we are not tapping the light within us as we think about these events—for the light would surely reveal to us the thread of cause and effect which led to these circumstances.

At the core of every event, person, social movement, and habit is an essence which is its primary motivating and sustaining force. This is its "soul." This soul, in turn, derives its life from a larger motivating force, which itself embodies an even greater authority and light. The light of a good idea may be quite strong, in other words, but the light of the archetypal pattern from which this good idea derives is even greater, as is the light of the divine creative will. The hierarchical nature of thinking impels us to continue searching for the most fundamental cause or origin of our ideas, inspirations, and direction. In this way, we learn to penetrate to the fullest source of divine light, and to seek out *the ultimate cause—the soul or essence—of every phenomenon of life.*

These five principles of esoteric life are not just a convenient way of examining the light, love, and will of God. They describe the way divine force itself acts. As we touch the light of God, therefore, and flood our mind with its illumination, it does not just reveal us for what we are and what we can become. Far more dynamically, it reshapes our personal energies of thought and our mental skills so that they begin to operate in harmony with these principles. As we cultivate these principles, we accelerate the process of becoming an effective agent of light—and love and will as well.

Little by little, we build a bridge of enlightened thought which becomes the vehicle for divine light to enter our mind and self-expression. We link earth with heaven through the medium of our mind, and thereby bring the light of heaven to earth for the benefit of all.

LOVING AS WE ARE LOVED

Love is the greatest of divine forces. The Christ repeatedly taught us that God *is* love—that is, the whole nature of God is summed up in the presence of divine love. It is therefore imperative to find divine love within ourself and learn to express it in the way we treat others, nurture our responsibilities, and approach life.

Not all love is divine love, however, and most people habitually confuse the many types of love, without realizing their error. They mistake fraternal love for divine love, or substitute personal affection or even the feeling of lust for the nobler qualities of goodwill, compassion, and benevolence. Some people even believe that such destructive attitudes as jealousy and animosity can be signs of love! Nevertheless, we are all moved by love; we respond to it and express it in one way or another. In some cases, our expression of love is very selfish, highlighting our personal needs. At other times, it may be altruistic, revealing some facet of the life of spirit. To the degree that we are selfish and protective of personal interests in our use of love, we bind ourself to earth and our earthly desires. But to the degree that we focus our love on divine ideas and the treasures of the kingdom of God, using it to help, nurture, and inspire others, we reveal heaven.

It can be difficult to separate our personal affection and devotion from the presence of divine love, yet this is precisely the distinction we must learn to make, if we are to tap the genuine source of divine love and incorporate it into our own self-expression. The reason for this difficulty is that the vast majority of people think of love purely as a function of their emotions and feelings. Their only experience of love has been at the level of the emotions, as they have exchanged affection, enthusiasm, and other feelings with loved ones, colleagues, and friends.

Divine love, however, is not an emotion; nor is it expressed as a good feeling. Divine love is the force which nurtures the growth of consciousness within all forms. As God pours out His love to us, for example, the nurturing force of this benevolence gently but powerfully summons us, as though we were drawn magnetically, to fulfill and express our divine design. As we learn to respond to this love, it heals that which has been misused, enriches that which is noble, and strengthens the bond between our higher and lower selves. It purifies, disciplines, and redeems the emotions, and helps the emotions reflect and serve divine love. Yet divine love is never just a feeling; it is the heart of our humanity. As we strive to tap the source of divine love within us, therefore, and express it in our daily life, we must be careful to go beyond the level of our feelings and contact the true source of nurturing goodwill and benevolence within us.

To put it classically, we must learn to love even as we are loved. We are loved by life itself—by God, by the Christ, and by our higher self or soul. Yet this is not the highly personal affection we usually label love. We are loved even if we have a poor self-image and feel ourself unworthy of love. We are loved even when we turn our back on divine life and plunge ourself into the material life. Yet because we fail to respond, we do not become aware of this love, or learn to express it. By contrast, when we seek divine love and strive to use it responsibly, we discover great depths to this love. Because God loves us, He nurtures and supports any of our plans and activities which is in harmony with His own plan. Because the Christ loves us, He adds His forgiveness and healing power to our humble efforts to forgive and help others. Because our higher self or soul loves us, it embraces the best within us and helps us grow. It leads us into new opportunities to grow.

As we are loved in these ways, we can best learn to express love by loving others, our work, and our personal destiny in similar ways—loving even as we are loved. Understanding this, it can then be very beneficial to examine the love of God in the light of the five principles of the esoteric perspective, so that we may acquire a better understanding of this source of divine life and force.

Life is multidimensional. Our emotions tend to react strongly to the imperfections and flaws in other people, making it difficult for us to express the feelings we call love to these individuals. Because life is multidimensional, however, we are able to rise above these reactions and identify with the spiritual essence and purpose within everyone and everything, regardless of how flawed they may appear. We can then love even as we are loved.

The enlightened parent, for example, finds it easy to love the essence of maturity in his or her child, even while the child is misbehaving and creating disturbances. Indeed, the parent's love for the spiritual potential of the child will probably motivate him or her to take corrective action, disciplining the child. The child will probably protest and resent this discipline, claiming that the parent does not love him anymore. Yet at the inner level, the parent has tapped and expressed the source of love.

There are many practical applications of multidimensionality. It lets us look beyond outer forms and enjoy the beauty and majesty of a Beethoven concerto, even when it is poorly performed. It similarly allows us to appreciate the love with which a child draws a birthday card for his or her parent, even though the finished card is apt to be awkward and not very well done.

When we love multidimensionally, we direct our love toward the perfect spiritual essence of our friends, our own talents, our work projects, and aspects of society, not because we approve of them in every aspect, *but because we are loved in the same way.* This love is not blind to imperfection, yet neither does it demand some impossible standard of perfection. Instead, it looks beyond the outer levels of events to behold the living force of divinity that is the heart of all phenomena.

The great value of loving in this way is that it lets us pursue our Father's business even in the midst of imperfection and opposition. This is no mere philosophical nicety, but an important facet of the great healing and nurturing force we call love. If we make too much of outer appearances, it is possible to blind ourself to the inner life which can change them. Even worse, too much concern about "the problem" can simply energize it. Unfortunately, it has become more popular to be a social critic than a healer of problems. Critics of society and humanity are hailed by the news media as great visionaries, yet the breadth and scope of their vision is generally remarkably narrow, defined by hysteria and etched in expediency. The true visionary is a much rarer species, as it demands the ability to look beyond the actual conditions of life and behold the ideal which needs to be honored. It takes spiritual love, not naïveté, to perceive and sustain this vision—a vision which can heal and build, because it embraces the creative potential of life as a real possibility, instead of rejecting and condemning the effort already made.

Our life exists within a greater life. The Apostle Paul referred to God as "the one in whom we live and move and have our being." Our very capacity to know love and respond to love, even as we are loved, is based on that fact—that the love of the One Life encompasses and embraces all things, including us. Therefore, this love can "endure all things," because it transcends all things.

This is a statement of great hope. Our human fears, doubts, and sadness may at times seem to overwhelm us, but we must keep in mind that there is a larger, spiritual force which can overwhelm them, if we but harness it. Our doubts, fears, and sadness can endure only as long as we feed and sustain them. But spiritual love endures forever, because it originates in the divine source of life. It is a permanent part of our spiritual being, unlike the temporary moods and feelings which tend to tyrannize us in daily life. It can therefore be called on to help us heal and redeem our doubts, fears, and sadness, replacing them with the "good fruit" of compassion, tolerance, affection, forgiveness, and faith.

If people could understand the principle of life existing within a greater life, they would be able to conquer the tyranny of negative emotions much more rapidly. Hostility, for example, is not really an isolated reaction to an obnoxious circumstance; in most cases, it is a habitual response to life. Hostile people carry with them a large storehouse of anger; as they encounter opposition, the anger rises up automatically and produces a hostile reaction. In this way, their hostility is a life within the larger life of their anger.

Just so, people who are habitually cynical and paranoid are apt to find fault with virtually everything. Yet the minor flaws they criticize rarely justify the excessive force of their cynicism. The real basis for their criticism lies in the greater storehouse of rejection and fear within their character.

In both of these examples, plentiful help is available, if they realize that there is a greater life than either their hostility or their pessimism. This is the greater life of the healing and nurturing love of their own spiritual self. People become hostile and cynical because their own personal resources of patience, forgiveness, confidence, and joy are not enough to meet the needs of some particular crisis, and they do not realize that there is any other source they can turn to. So they retreat into defensiveness. But there is a greater source—the love of our spiritual self. Whenever we feel lacking in forgiveness ourself, we can call on the divine love of the greater life to fill us with goodwill. Whenever we feel lacking in joy ourself, we can call on the divine love of the greater life to fill us with a renewed delight in living. In this way, we can overwhelm the pettiness of negative feelings, rather than being overwhelmed by them.

Of course, it is not necessary to have great hostility or fears in order to draw on this greater life. Anyone who aspires to know and express the love of God can tap this resource. It is a simple matter of activating our individual capacity for kindness, gentleness, forgiveness, affection, cheerfulness, and devotion. As we love others and life through these refined and spiritualized expressions of our emotions, resting in the knowledge that our life exists within a greater life, we will find that we are loved even as we have learned to love.

Life is hierarchical. Spirit often calls upon the personality to make sacrifices of time, comfort, or money in order to pursue goals which are important to us spiritually. If we think only in terms of what the personality wants or finds comfortable, we will probably refuse to make most of these sacrifices—except those which help us look good in the eyes of others. But if we are able to love the larger purposes involved and understand that it is the vast drama of human growth and service which gives meaning and richness to our personal life, then we will find it easier to express our love in ways that honor our spiritual design and dignity. Even in the spiritually dedicated person, the path to our most cherished goals is often strewn with all kinds of hardships. If we give up at the second or third difficulty, we will fail at nearly everything. But if our devotion to the goal is strong, then our love for the right result can override the distress in the hardships we must endure to achieve this goal. As we learn to love hierarchically, we are able to separate meaningful goals and endeavors from lesser ones. As a result, we learn to focus our sustaining and protecting love intelligently, rather than indulgently.

In addition, people we love and care about may at times do and say things which offend or disappoint us. It may occasionally be difficult to restrain the impulse to snap back at them or return their angry words. But if our love for their inner being is strong, it will establish a hierarchy for our priorities in this relationship. Our knowledge of what is truly important will be strong enough to help us discipline our hurt feelings and respond not with anger but with patience, tolerance, and forgiveness. In this way, our spiritual bond of love is able to overwhelm and neutralize temporary negative reactions, and we remain attuned to the truly important elements of life.

The universality of life. Many people distort love with heavy feelings of jealousy and selfishness. They want to possess the object of their love and are envious of anyone who might want to take it away from them—or anyone who might have what they want but have not yet attained. The spiritual person, however, has learned to practice detachment from the objects of love. He has learned that the highest form of love is to love the intangible, universal realities of the inner life in all things, not the physical objects of earth. And so, he loves the basic goodness and spiritual qualities in others, and does what he can to nurture them. He rejoices in the achievements and good fortune of others, for he sees it as proof that there is an inherent, universal goodness about life.

It is the universality of life that helps us master this impersonal but dedicated use of divine love. At first, people who are addicted to the highly personal focus of emotions and feelings scorn this expression of love, but it is not actually that hard to learn. Most people, after all, are able to love the universal qualities of beauty and order in nature, even though they cannot and do not possess nature personally. Most of us can also learn to love people for what they are rather than for what they can do for us. We can learn to respect the fact that there is virtue and talent in everyone, if we but look for it. And we can learn to appreciate that there is a universal abundance of intelligence, cheerfulness, patience, and courage available to us, through the divine source of love.

As we learn to love in this way, we depersonalize our human affections. We do not love spiritually until we can love without attachment and without thought of personal benefit or comfort coming from the object of our affection. Nor can we heal, nurture, or support spiritually—the practical expressions of love—until we can do so without personal expectations. As always, we must love even as we are loved, and we are loved for our potential to act as an agent of the divine plan.

The spiritual value of universality to our ability to love is greatest as we learn to sense the undercurrent of goodwill and benevolence which permeates all of life and all people. This undercurrent of goodwill is the wavelength of our kinship with all others and with life as a whole. As we learn to recognize it even in the most humble aspect of life, we tap the source of divine love within us and strengthen its presence in our own awareness.

Life is continuous. It is easy to love God and our fellow man in the abstract; it is quite another matter to sustain goodwill, tolerance, and affection in the face of unpleasant events or angry, childish, or irrational behavior by others. Our personal feelings are often fluid and our reactions can be difficult to control, yet spirit loves with a constancy that knows no end. As we learn that divine love is continuous and does not perish, even under the force of our own immaturity, we will find it easier to mobilize the strength to persevere in our goodwill.

The Apostle Paul explained this most eloquently when he wrote in Romans 8:38: "Nothing can separate us from the love of God; neither death nor life, neither angels or other heavenly rulers; neither the present nor the future; neither the world above nor the world below." The constancy of divine love in our life can be broken only by our own forgetfulness and a willful descent into despair, fear, and anger. But as we learn to act with constancy in our expression of love, and from this become acquainted with the constancy of divine love, we can lift up our eyes and our heart to behold this great and eternal benevolent power in our midst—in our *life*—serving as a continual source of renewal and healing for us all.

To the spiritual aspirant, the heart of developing the continuity of love lies in increasing our capacity to act with goodwill. It is relatively easy to attune ourself to heaven and fill our heart with goodwill; the challenge lies in translating this goodwill into an active expression on earth, so that as we draw to ourself impatience, distrust, disharmony, and other problems—from within ourself, within others, or within society as a whole—we transform them with a steady expression of goodwill. This kind of goodwill cannot be sustained unless we maintain our faith, devotion, and reverence for the love of God on a regular, on-going basis. As divine love is an inexhaustible resource, we should be able to demonstrate that our love and goodwill will not evaporate in the face of difficulty.

As we master these five principles in the expression of love, we come to a new appreciation of the statement that "God is love." These simple words speak volumes, for they tell us that God is alive, dynamic, and intimately involved in His creation. He nurtures the good within us all and provides us with the resources we need to fulfill our potential and make our contribution. There is no limit to the measure of love that we can draw on for our own self-expression; the only limits are those we impose. And as we learn to love in this fashion, we come face to face with God and discover by experience what it means to love even as we have been loved.

ACTING WITH WILL

The third great source of divine power is the will. It is also the least understood. In many respects, however, the mystery of the will is overrated. It should be obvious that when God creates, He acts with purpose. This purpose might also be called divine intent or divine will. The will is that force which activates creation, sustains it, and impels it to reach its destined fulfillment. It is the source of all action, growth, and achievement in life. It is the ultimate authority and motivation for all change, progress, and development.

The problem is that even though many people have a great deal of experience acting willfully, few have any real experience acting with will—meaning divine purpose. Yet since this is the source of all meaningful forward movement, either in our own life or in the life of a business, society, or nation, there is great wisdom in learning to act with will.

First, we must understand that the will of God has nothing to do with wrath, anger, or displeasure. For century after century, we have tried to use the will of God as an almighty club with which to destroy our enemies. People have called on the will of God to defend them, to protect them, and to punish their adversaries. In their own lives, they have tried to imitate divine will by being assertive, stubborn, and highly opinionated. Yet the will of God does not operate in these ways.

The will of God is not something we imitate in our life; it is something we try to act in harmony with. It is not something to question; if it is the will of God that the sky should be blue on sunny days, it is immaterial if we should prefer green. As Pope put it, "Whatever is, is right." It does not require our blessing—or even our understanding. But we are meant to cooperate with it.

Few spectacles are sillier or more pathetic than a prideful man or woman defying the will of God. Yet when we do not understand our proper role in life, this can indeed happen. There is a strong tendency in our human nature to rebel against authority. And nothing feeds the pride of a weak person more than the notion that he or she is rebelling against *the ultimate authority*—God's will.

This is a game that only we play, however. God has nothing to do with it. The will of God was determined at the onset of creation. If we want to live our life out of harmony with divine will, so be it, but it is a personal choice and nothing more. It is certainly not an act of defiance—just an act of stupidity. The better option, of course, is to act in harmony with divine intent as much as we can.

Some people will protest that they do not know enough about the divine will to act in harmony with it. This is usually just a clever excuse, however, for it is seldom difficult to determine the major elements of divine intent for our life. If we are blessed with various skills, it should be obvious that it is the divine will to develop these skills and apply them productively in life. If we are married, it should be clear that it is the divine will to make this marriage an expression of divine love. If we have been blessed with children, it should be obvious that it is the divine will to help these children become mature, productive adults. The major conditions of our life tell us so much about the divine will that no one should ever have to ponder, "What is the divine intent for me?"

If nothing else, we can always remember that the constant challenge of the spiritual person is not just to find, but also to *reveal the presence of God in all that he does*. Every opportunity that comes to us is a chance to translate some quality or force of the divine life into a new expression on earth, no matter how mundane or trivial the activity may be. It is not just in moments of creative triumph that we fulfill the will of God. Far more commonly, the intent of God is expressed in the way we approach the routines and common experiences of daily life. If we bring peace on earth and express goodwill toward everyone we deal with, then who is to say we are not fulfilling the will of God?

All human activity can be infused with the intent and purpose of divine life, if we so choose. Even such dull routines as housecleaning, mowing the lawn, or driving to work can become significant, if we approach them as ways to sustain the momentum of our more important activities. Housework, for instance, becomes more significant to us as we learn to view it as a way of creating a wholesome atmosphere of order and neatness for our family.

The nature of the will and how we can add it to our daily activities, thereby enriching our self-expression, stands out more clearly by examining the five principles of the esoteric perspective. These principles, when fully understood and worked out, give us a whole new understanding of what it means to be a human being, alive on the planet and involved in the unfoldment of the divine plan.

Life is multidimensional. There are many times when we may feel trapped in limited circumstances—an unhappy marriage, an unfulfilling job, or some restrictive obligation. But chances are very good that this limitation is *only our perception* of the problems and opportunities at hand. Someone else might be able to take the very same job that we hold and find great fulfillment in it, by approaching it with more enthusiasm, a deeper love of excellence, and a greater amount of intelligence than we have invested in it. It is almost always a trap to assume that the circumstances of our life are limited or uninspiring.

Because life is multidimensional, there are many inner perspectives and possibilities to any circumstance that the average person leaves unexplored. One of the most important of these is the divine design for achievement or perfection. If we can make the effort to tap the divine intent for our marriage, our work, or any other circumstance, it will be almost impossible to be bored or trapped by them. At the very least, these "limiting" circumstances can teach us to move and act more gracefully, with greater patience, optimism, enthusiasm, and kindness toward others, so that we come to appreciate the immense potential of even the most trivial aspects of life. Far more likely, we will tap a level of spiritual quality and purpose which exalts the meaning and effectiveness of our marriage, work, or commitment.

Because we do not usually approach life multidimensionally, we often take too much of our life for granted. Failing to contemplate the divine intent behind our work, or education, or marriage, we overlook the lessons we are learning, the skills we are developing, or the maturity we are gaining. We also tend to overlook the need to involve the full force of our personality and character in whatever we do. It is as though we were an artist who mechanically reproduces a landscape on his canvas with technical precision but no insight or emotion. The result is a flat, dull painting. A master artist, by contrast, would seek to add his own enthusiasm and joy, his insights and perspectives on life, and his devotion to beauty and gracefulness to everything he paints. The result will be a landscape or portrait which is something more than just the scene or person portrayed; it is a revelation of the inner dimensions which inspired and guided the artist.

Just so, the work we do is meant to reveal the inner dimensions of our character as well as our talents and time spent. Our relationships with others are meant to reveal and embody our deepest capacities to express goodwill, compassion, and friendship. Our spiritual service is meant to express the most profound measure of commitment, as well as a certain knowledge of just what kind of service is truly needed. When we act in life in a cold and perfunctory way, as though we were nothing more than a robot, we fall far short of our potential. We need to charge our awareness of the multidimensionality of life with a fresh jolt of divine will, and rediscover what it means to express *our full range of humanity* in everything we do.

Our life exists within a larger life. Many people seem to move through life as though they must tiptoe discreetly around every possible pitfall or challenge. They carefully maintain what is, basically, a defensive attitude toward almost every aspect of life. They are more interested in making it through the potential threats of daily life without any hassles than they are in being a constructive force or agent of God.

But spirit is not especially interested in our defensiveness. Spirit wants us to be a force of divine blessing—a helpful, constructive influence on the life around us. If we can appreciate that we draw our true purpose in living from a greater and more powerful life than our personality and body, then it is possible to break out of the trap of defensiveness. We need to realize that the skills of self-expression and creative talent are mastered only if we are willing to risk investing ourself in innovative projects, new growth, and opportunities.

There is a time and a place for defending that which we know to be right and noble, but the habit of defensiveness seldom serves this end. In most cases, it just becomes an excuse for not investing our time and talents in worthwhile pursuits. Risks are always hard to take. But if we know that we truly do exist as a life within a greater life, then we have the full resources of this greater life to call upon and express in the sensible risks that we take. And on those rare occasions when we are called to defend that which we value, the full range of the greater life will also be there to support us.

Life is hierarchical. A common danger to every spiritual student is the distraction of crises and obligations which eat up our time and energies throughout the day. Sometimes these distractions are very subtle and come in the form of too many options, too many opportunities. At other times, the distractions arrive in the form of too many problems, major and minor. Yet the danger is the same in either case. We try to do too many things at the same time—some irrelevant tasks, some necessary ones, and almost all of them poorly managed in the panic of crises and deadlines. The result is usually a series of mistakes which have to be corrected, a great deal of frustration, and terrible fatigue.

This problem tends to happen because we are still centered mainly in the life of the personality. The personality is concerned primarily with whatever the problem of the moment happens to be. As we identify more with spirit, however, and learn to act in harmony with its enlightened perspective, we quickly begin to understand what our true priorities are meant to be. We are able to see what problems are serious and need attention—and which are trivial and can be ignored. We are also able to judge which opportunities are in harmony with the intent of the soul—and which can better be handled by others. This is because God truly has become the center of our world, and out of this center we have learned to act in daily life with the maximum measure of guidance, love, and strength. We work from the highest priority to the lowest, rather than from the most immediate to the most abstract.

Life is universal. One of the great mistakes most aspirants make in trying to align themselves with will is the temptation to think individually—for example, in terms of "God's will for me." Divine will is a broad force which comes to us universally, not personally—as the collective purpose of humanity. There is much that we can learn about applying the will individually, but we must always remember that life is universal. God's will is basically the same for all of us, but each of us individually needs to find and establish our own place in the divine scheme. As we act in life, therefore, we must always remember to act in harmony with the small and large groups to which we belong, and not just as an isolated individual.

We share life, and therefore must share responsibility. In an office, if one person is upset, it can infect the mood of the whole office in a very short period of time. Conversely, if one person is full of enthusiasm and creative ideas, it can rapidly inspire and motivate others around him.

As a spiritual aspirant, we need to recognize that we are part of mankind, and that the way we think, feel, and act can dishonor or inspire humanity. If we are selfish and parasitic, we deplete human culture and its resources. But if we are productive and generous in thought, emotions, and deed, we add to the abundance of earth. We are not an island unto ourself—in a powerful way, everything we do becomes our contribution to humanity and God. Whether our contribution is trivial or significant, helpful or harmful, depends to a large degree on how much we act with divine will.

Working as an agent of God requires us to act as a universal being—a person who knows that the roots of his consciousness are in the mind and heart of God, and that the value of our work lies in helping fulfill God's plan for all humanity.

Life is continuous. It is often difficult to sustain our efforts in life, especially when the outlook for success is bleak. For many of us, indeed, this is the greatest challenge we face in finding heaven on earth and linking earth with heaven. Saddled with the burden of a lifelong illness or a persistent feeling of inadequacy, it can be very difficult to summon the strength and faith we need to continue. But the spiritual person learns that even though the personality may experience cycles of stagnation and hardship, our spiritual essence remains constant. Its strength does not waver, even when ours does, any more than the strength of love or beauty or joy or any of the treasures of spirit waver. Divine life endures and continues to fulfill the plan of God. Knowing this, then we, too, can meet whatever burdens life gives us and carry them with us along our chosen path—with patience, strength, love, and wisdom. In this way, we make a powerful link with divine will—not through the exercising of our personal will but through the continuous application of faith, persistence, and dedication. We also demonstrate that the power of heaven is strong enough to defeat even the greatest obstacles on earth.

There is much we have yet to learn about acting with will. For most people, the challenge is simply to learn to act, rather than react in life. Acting implies a sense of purpose or conscious intent. Yet most people go through life without acting at all, just blindly reacting to what happens to them. As a result, they get caught in a web of their own weaving.

Creative expression, however, requires something greater than reactiveness. We must therefore never underrate our ability to act. Each act spins an opportunity; each act gives us a chance to reveal heaven on earth. We can fill our acts with selfishness and greed—or we can fill them with goodwill, harmony, wisdom, joy, generosity, courage, faith, cooperation, and patience.

To act with will implies that we strive to become a perfect channel for God's purpose and life.

EXPERIENCING GOD

It is the ability to put these five esoteric principles to work in our life in these ways which makes us an inner-directed person—not the amount of scripture we have memorized or the volume of esoteric trivia we have absorbed. It is our own livingness which should be considered our finest and most important source of spiritual inspiration, because our own life is our best and most direct link with heaven.

One of the primary responsibilities of the esoteric student is to build a structure of understanding, motives, values, attitudes, and abilities which aligns him to God. In essence, this structure in consciousness becomes a bridge of enlightened qualities of thought, creativity, goodwill, and habits linking us with the kingdom of heaven within us. Once this bridge is built, the treasures of heaven can be poured out on earth. The abstract and universal love of God can be translated into nurturing and supportive love for the divine potential of all things on earth. Inspiration can be translated into innovative solutions to problems on earth. And the will of God can be channeled to motivate us to act in enlightened ways.

The proper study and use of esoteric forces, therefore, is to build this bridge—the bridge that will link earth to heaven, heaven to earth in our own life. The enlightened person knows that it does no good to have studied spiritual facts and esoteric principles unless they can be applied to practical ends. Likewise, he knows that it does little good to theorize about divine love—or even contact it—unless it can be expressed in his daily life. So he strives to learn as much about the nature of divine life and force as he can. This requires something more than mere belief and a willingness to obey God. It takes hard work and constant effort, as we seek to build up the sensitivity, responsiveness, competence, goodwill, wisdom, joy, and patience that we need to become a fitting agent of spirit. *Building this bridge of enlightened attitudes and divine qualities is the responsibility of each person.*

The enlightened person will therefore look everywhere for the presence and influence of God, but most of all, he will look within himself. We cannot properly honor God if we do not understand ourself. It is not enough to study God as He embraces a mountain range, yet ignore divine purpose and will in our own life. Nor is it enough to believe that God is all wise and all knowing, then act with ignorance and prejudice. It is not enough to proclaim that *God is love,* then express anger and hostility in our dealings with others.

We must experience God. We must look for God not just in heaven, but also on earth—and we must find Him. We must look for God not just in divine ideas, but also in our own thinking—and express the light of His plan. We must look for God not just in divine love, but also in our own heart—and nurture His plan. We must look for God not just in miracles and signs, but also in our own constructive, helpful acts—and reveal His nature through all that we do.

If we experience God in these ways, then the beauty of our design as a human being will be revealed. We will be a child of earth and a child of heaven in one—a multidimensional, universal being through whom God can nurture, sustain, and enlighten life on earth. We will be able to stand in the light and proclaim:

I am the Symbolic and the Real,
A fragment of heaven come to earth;
The image of the Great One's seal,
I am the Symbolic and the Real.

Through tests and triumphs I reveal
Humanity's destiny and worth;
I am the Symbolic and the Real,
A fragment of heaven come to earth.

Harnessing
Esoteric Traditions

Since divine intelligence pervades all of life, the proper study of almost everything will lead us back to God. Some of these avenues of study have proven so effective that they have become traditions. The following essay examines the primary esoteric traditions and how they can be harnessed to tap into the power, love, and wisdom of God.

THE MANY PATHS TO GOD

If we are in Washington, D.C., and wish to travel to San Francisco, we are not limited to just one route. There are many effective ways we can travel across country, depending upon our purpose, interest, budget, and whim. The most obvious choice may be to hop in our car and follow the interstate system. But we may be more scenic-minded and choose to take country roads meandering through small towns. The trip will probably take twice as long, but may prove to be far more exciting and relaxing. Of course, if we are truly adventurous, we might leave the car at home and hitchhike, taking whatever route chance dictates to us. At the opposite extreme, we could choose to fly. We could also travel by train or bus. There are many choices open to us.

The same is true as we travel the spiritual path. There is One God, but many different pathways we can take to reunite with the Godhead within us. Some of these pathways are as well-trodden as the major interstates and commercial airline routes; these would be the major religions of the world. Others are less well-known, but equally suitable—the great myths of world culture, certain mystical traditions, and systems of divination such as the I Ching or astrology. Properly used, each one of these paths leads us to God—and likewise serves as a channel through which the power, wisdom, and love of God flows into the earth plane. No one way is "right" or "best"—each serves its unique purpose. The choice is ours. Which path we choose is not nearly as important as choosing to follow it with faith and wisdom, *until we reach our destination!*

It is unfortunate that so many people have been brainwashed into believing that God has prepared *only one way* for us to discover His grace, love, and wisdom. If we humans are smart enough to have developed an almost infinite number of ways to travel from Washington to San Francisco, then why should we

71.

assume that God, the greatest Intelligence in the universe, a Being who surely understands the pettiness, ignorance, and competitiveness of human nature, would insist that every member of the human race follow the exact same path to Him? The very notion blasphemes God's wisdom and love.

This is just a matter of common sense. It is silly to go anywhere by car without a spare tire. It is equally foolish to use a computer without making backup copies of our files. And we would never dream of launching a spacecraft without some kind of backup for virtually every major system on board, in case one fails. In our technological society, we have taken this kind of redundancy for granted; we know it is the intelligent thing to do.

It is likewise a good idea to understand that God does not force us all into one single mold. The facts are everywhere around us. Ours is a world of many nations, races, and creeds. God created us in this diversity. We earn our living by practicing thousands of different occupations, crafts, and professions. There are scores of different cultures throughout the world, with hundreds of languages and dialects, thousands of customs, and many different ways of looking at life. Since God is both omnipresent and omnipotent, it is only rational to assume that this rich diversity of the human race serves the divine plan—in fact, was *inspired* by the divine plan. No other conclusion makes sense.

It is therefore just an extension of common sense to recognize that there are many pathways by which we can return to the Godhead, and many channels through which God reaches out and touches us, in our daily lives. No one religion or culture has a monopoly on God; if it did, then that particular religion or culture would be greater than God, which is absurd. Each major religion and culture develops its own customs and traditions leading back to God. For the people of that religion or culture, these customs and traditions represent the surest and most stimulating way to discover God and His involvement in our daily life. But each of these spiritual traditions must be recognized for the contribution it makes. They are all valid traditions.

To understand why we have developed these traditions, we must realize that part of our collective purpose and destiny is to become, as a nation, race, or culture, an effective channel for divine expression. Only in this way can we fulfill the plan of God. First, we must come to know God in a deep and intimate way; then we must learn to express His divine qualities and attributes in our own life. As the leading members of any race, culture, or nation learn to do this individually, they must then extend the scope of their work to stimulate the entire group toward spiritual expression. In this way, we participate with God in the work of evolution—and likewise strengthen the spiritual traditions of our particular group.

These traditions evolve through the interaction of spiritual people with the love and wisdom of God. None of these pathways, not even the great religions, is solely a creation of divine will and intelligence. God, in other words, does not come *to us* so much as He comes *through us*. We are the agents of divine life and tradition here on earth; God *walks on earth through the cooperation of responsive human beings who are dedicated to revealing the divine plan.* Indeed, history is filled with records of these agents of God, who have revealed the wisdom and beauty of the divine plan in their teachings and works. Some have been the major leaders and teachers of the great world religions. Others have been active in philosophy, the arts, esoteric sciences, or even government. Still others have been enlightened people who left no record other than their individual influence on colleagues and friends. Their methods of expression have varied with their individuality, but there is one thread common to all: each has been a human agent through which the power, love, and wisdom of God has been revealed to us.

The bigots and fanatics of the world will reject this basic premise, of course. They have been taught that their particular tradition, whatever it is, is the one true revelation of God and that it came directly from God, untouched by human hands or vocal chords. But their own scriptures do not support their wild claims. It is clear that the Holy Bible was written by human beings, not by divine dictation; each of the Gospels, for instance, is plainly attributed to its author. These truths have come to us through human and divine *cooperation*—not through direct intervention of God. Accepting this fact does not in any way diminish the value of the Bible; in fact, it serves to enhance it. The Bible becomes something more than a collection of two-thousand-year-old stories; it becomes an important document that shows us how to reveal the presence and wisdom of God in our own lives!

The problem with any of these traditions, of course, is that they can be so easily dominated by fanatics and bigots. As centuries pass, the original light that shone through the tradition becomes dimmed by the narrowness and pettiness of the dark side of human nature. The original purpose of the tradition fades and is replaced by self-serving motives. The original rites degenerate into lifeless liturgy. The initial reverence for spirit is lost and is replaced by a fierce idolatry of sacred texts and rituals.

Actually, the original tradition still remains and is just as powerful as ever. But it has been obscured by a "shadow tradition" of the same name. It is this shadow tradition which is commonly practiced by the general public. The original tradition is preserved only in the minds and hearts of the spiritually-dedicated. Quite often, the shadow traditions end up advocating and enshrining the exact opposite of the basic tenets of the original tradition. But this does not trouble the bigots and fanatics.

The terms "esoteric" and "exoteric" can be helpful in making this distinction. The word "esoteric" means the inner truth; the word "exoteric" means the outer truth. An esoteric spiritual tradition is therefore the original, true, undiluted tradition as first revealed through one or more agents of God. An exoteric spiritual tradition is the shadow tradition which arises as the original truths become watered down, adapted, politicized, and made palatable to millions of people in a given culture.

It should be understood that an exoteric spiritual tradition can lead us part way on our path to God—but it can just as easily mislead us. Roman Catholicism, for instance, has helped many people find their way to God, but it has also been responsible for spreading an inordinate amount of guilt and fear, which hampers the effort to grow in spirit. An esoteric spiritual tradition, by contrast, will tend to take us directly to the heart of divine life, if we use it in its pure form, without distortion. This is the great message left to us by the lives of the Catholic saints. Even though the exoteric form of Catholicism has been weakened and polluted, the esoteric heart of it still remains vibrant, true, and responsive to all sincere inquiries.

All esoteric traditions have been hidden by their exoteric counterparts in this way. The Kabalah has been suffocated by centuries of Jewish theology. The Tarot has been demeaned by thousands of years in the hands of fortune tellers. Even mythology has not escaped unharmed, as it has been consigned to the safekeeping of academics who have little imagination and less spiritual insight.

Exoteric traditions vary tremendously. This is not the case with the original, esoteric traditions, however. At their heart, they are in harmony with one another, *because they are all inspired by the same divine sources.* For this reason, the intelligent person views all of these traditions as different parts of the same whole. The routes vary, but the destination is the same in each case.

As a result, if one channel is blocked by the sclerosis of too many laws and rituals, another can still serve as the conduit of God's redeeming love. If one source of divine guidance is blocked by the incompetence or ignorance of the present-day guardians of that system, divine inspiration can still find its way to earth through other means. Humanity is never left to fend for itself, no matter how corrupt or degraded any one exoteric tradition may become.

The reason for having a number of esoteric traditions is underscored by the basic needs of humanity itself. Not all human cultures have the same needs for divine enrichment. Some cultures, especially in the East, are rich in goodwill and gentleness, but weak in wisdom. Their traditions need to be designed to emphasize divine intelligence. Other cultures, primarily in the West, are well organized around intelligent principles, but are weak in goodwill, forgiveness, and charity. Their traditions tend to emphasize the character and strength of divine love. More primitive cultures, which lack a strong intellectual and linguistic foundation, will embrace more mystical traditions, as is often the case among the tribes of Africa and native America.

It is also important to realize that civilization and human nature do not remain static. The evolution of ideas is continual, even when it goes unrecognized. And so, the new revelations of one era eventually become infused into the mainstream of collective human values, thoughts, and behavior. Society accepts what has been revealed, even though it may require thousands of years. In this way, another phase of the plan of God is fulfilled, making way for the appearance of another new revelation of divine wisdom, love, or joy. A new religion, system of divination, or other esoteric tradition emerges, and the process begins anew. Divine intelligence, working through human agents of light, reveals to us a new understanding of the laws of subtle energies, a new potential for contact with the angelic kingdom, or a fresh realization of the esoteric workings of human psychology.

Just as humanity evolves, so does each individual spiritual person. In the early stages of aspiration, identification with the exoteric teachings of a single tradition may be all the individual can handle. But as our commitment to spiritual growth deepens, we begin to see the inadequacies of any exoteric approach to life. We invoke a greater understanding of the esoteric principles of life, and are led by our own higher intelligence to the study of a system most appropriate to us. Eventually, we begin to realize that all of these esoteric systems describe just one basic core of truth—the plan of God. Different cultures, races, nations, and temperaments need to work on differing facets of the same truth—but all paths converge and become one eventually.

The person who surveys the vast range of esoteric traditions and sees only the differences, none of the similarities, has no real understanding of the plan of God. Such a person is absorbed in his or her own separativeness and biases. The truth is that *all esoteric traditions are compatible with one another, for the simple reason that they all have their origins in the wisdom, love, and power of God!* Hinduism, Buddhism, and Christianity all reveal the same divine life, even though they are tailored for differing cultures. The Tarot, the I Ching, and astrology all are based on similar archetypal forces, although each has its own scope of influence. This is not just a matter of philosophical speculation. It is a fact that has been demonstrated repeatedly by God-conscious people, who have found that they can use any of these systems to reach the Godhead. These are people who commute to heaven every day of their lives, and so know the journey extremely well.

Moreover, there is a very good reason why the spiritual person should become equally at home with a wide variety of these esoteric traditions. The way to God is not just the way of faith and love. To become a spiritual person, we must exercise many different spiritual "muscles" and learn many different skills. Faith and love are important strengths. But wisdom, joy, self-control, creativity, and service are also of great importance. While some esoteric traditions focus primarily on the wisdom of God, others emphasize the love of God, while still others stress service and right living. Some will help us deal with the struggle between our human and spiritual natures, while others will attune us to the beauty of nature and the inner forces of the angelic kingdom. Each system is designed to fit a particular culture and time. It is absurd to think that any one esoteric system alone (even a religion) is all that we ever need; it is not only rude but also self-deceiving to try to limit God in this way!

Christianity, for instance, stresses the need to express divine qualities in the way we live—in particular, God's love. Yet it tends to neglect the inner side of our relation to God. Hinduism, on the other hand, provides a rich set of teachings on how to establish and enrich our contact with the God within us. Yet Hinduism tends to neglect the need to demonstrate divine love and wisdom through good works. So the weaknesses of Hinduism as practiced are the very strengths of Christianity as practiced, and vice-versa.

The problem facing us all, of course, is to make sure that we study the true, esoteric tradition, and not fall into the traps of the shadow, exoteric tradition associated with it. While the esoteric tradition of Christianity is rich in good works and service, for example, its exoteric tradition is marred by bigots and fanatics who practice outright malice and curse those who dare oppose them. While the esoteric tradition of Buddhism emphasizes the need to liberate ourselves from the pain of materialism, the exoteric expression of the same religion often teaches its followers to practice dedicated mindlessness and passiveness, which is not a liberation at all.

Other esoteric traditions suffer in the same way. While the esoteric structure of the Tarot is a solid structure of archetypal thought, the common exoteric use of this venerable system is mired in foolishness. While the esoteric tradition of the zodiac is a key to divine intelligence, its common exoteric practice is filled with superstition, error, and nonsense.

To harness the power of these esoteric traditions, we must recognize snobbery and arrogance for what they are, and not be intimidated by them. Religion does not have an exclusive franchise on God, either the worship of God or the revelation of God's plan. Science, charities, and enlightened governments have often done far more to point the way to God and reveal the divine plan than religion. Astrology and the I Ching are generally far more accurate oracles for divine revelation than most priests, rabbis, and ministers.

But religion is not the only tradition guilty of arrogance and snobbery. The "high priests" and "priestesses" of mythology, the Kabalah, or the Tarot are often just as bigoted and dogmatic as the most cocksure Bible-banging preacher. It is silly to devote one's life to expounding the wisdom in fables and mythology, yet overlook the truth in the parables of Jesus. It is also just as stupid to reject the dogma of religion, then turn about and create dogma of one's own.

So let us develop the true spirit of the dedicated traveler along the spiritual path, who knows there is just one destination worth reaching, but a multitude of paths by which to make the journey. If we are making the journey to heaven for the first time, we need to concentrate on just one path. But as we open up contact with spirit and find ourself making the journey every day of our life, it makes good sense to become adept at traveling as many paths as we can.

Even more importantly, if humanity is to establish a fuller contact with divinity, we must learn to respect the rich treasures we have been given in our esoteric traditions. We must stop fighting and quibbling over which tradition is the best, and learn to put them all to work for us. For as we do, we honor God, Who is at the heart of all these traditions.

THE MAJOR TRADITIONS

We tend to think of experience as a sequence of random events which intertwine to create the thread of our life. If we end up unhappy, we probably blame our experiences for it; if only we had chosen a different branching of the path twenty years ago, everything might have been better. If we end up successful, we may think ourself blessed. In either event, we probably do not comprehend the real meaning of experience at any level deeper than the old cliché, "Live and learn."

Mankind as a whole lives and learns, too. It condenses the lessons it learns from experience into traditions, so that succeeding generations can benefit from the gains of prior ones. Not all of these traditions are based on wisdom; some are downright foolish. But they are based on experience and the response of our culture to it.

Spiritual traditions are those that relate us to the life of spirit. The wise ones are the esoteric, pure traditions. These speak to us of the love, wisdom, beauty, and joy of God. They tell us how to discover this love, wisdom, beauty, and joy in our own lives; they also show us how to express these qualities on our own— how to become an agent of divine life. The lesser spiritual traditions are the exoteric ones. They tend to tell us more about the confusion and weaknesses of human nature than they do about God.

Every valid esoteric tradition can enrich our life in some special way. To believe otherwise is to cheat ourself of some facet of divine life. We may choose to believe, for example, that the Tarot is just a game, whereas Christianity is *a way of life*, but we are just succumbing to the snobbery of exotericism. The Tarot is a complex structure which can reveal a good deal more about the divine plan than most standard Christian theology ever has.

Some of these esoteric traditions emphasize the ethics of spiritual growth. Others reveal the mechanism of divine intelligence. Still others focus on the need for self-purification in preparing our human nature to receive the divine outpouring. Others explain how divine forces interact with us in daily life, sometimes in unexpected and stressful ways, but always for our greater good.

Collectively, these esoteric traditions give us a complete picture of divine life in and around us—our divine potential, the nature of the spiritual path, the problems of redemption, the struggle of transcendence, and the nature of enlightened living. These insights may not be immediately apparent to the casual student, but they are there for those who have the eyes to see.

There are three basic groupings of these traditions: the major religions, occult traditions, and cultural traditions. Within each of these groups, there are four or five primary traditions which help humanity understand the life of God, and serve as vehicles through which the light and love of God pour into the earth plane. The special value of each of these traditions can be described as follows.

The Great Religions. Centuries of fanaticism and righteous bigotry, not to mention outright warfare and terrorism, have often tarnished these traditions. Yet the roots of all religions lie in the love and wisdom of God. No matter how much we may be tempted to condemn all religions for their exoteric excesses and sins, we must remember that within the outer shell there is a tremendous measure of light. This light is expressed in different ways by different religions, but the light is the same in all cases.

Hinduism. The great value of Hinduism is that it provides a comprehensive set of teachings about how to align our human awareness with divine consciousness. It gives us specific techniques we can use to find God—through self-control, prayer and meditation, and enlightened self-expression. These techniques show us how to turn our attention inward, quiet the emotions and mind, release our sense of selfhood to spirit, and transcend to a higher state of consciousness. Many of these techniques are spelled out in detail in the Sutras of Patanjali (see *The Light Within Us*).

Another Hindu text, *The Bhagavad-Gita,* provides us with the allegory of Arjuna, the story of every spiritual seeker trying to understand the nature of God and how to apply it to real life situations. Just prior to engaging in battle on the fields of Kurukshetra, Arjuna inquires of his master, who represents the wisdom of God in this story, if it is proper to fight his own kinsmen. It is clear that Arjuna's real struggle is between his human nature and the divine plan. The battle that is about to transpire is just the outer symbol of the inner confrontation, a confrontation each of us must learn to deal with as we progress on the path.

The esoteric value of Hinduism is that it teaches us that God is an omniscient, omnipotent, impersonal force which dwells within all visible life. Humanity is but one of many forms of life created by God, no more or less divine than a lump of clay. But unlike clay, humans have the opportunity to know God consciously and find union with the divine. Hinduism therefore puts the emphasis on developing the inner powers of consciousness. So long as we are focused exclusively on the physical plane, we will be a victim of the grand illusion. We will discount the real importance of God. But as we discover that God is the only true reality, our inner senses open up to us a vast range of subtle realms. We are meant to master these inner realms, so that we may achieve complete union with God.

Buddhism. The Buddha is a great Avatar who embodied the wisdom aspect of God. He presented fresh revelations about the nature of an enlightened relationship with God and the enlightened way to conduct ourself in daily life. Worship in Buddhism is not so much a formal ritual as it is a way of living in the context of the omnipresence of God. The Buddha stressed that it is our personal responsibility to live in harmony with the divine order and light of God.

The Buddha taught that life on earth is inherently full of suffering, because we usually choose to identify with our physical and emotional sensations—the world of senses, the passions of the body, and our continual tendency to dwell in the smallness and shallowness of the material world. In other words, we value that which is impermanent and illusory, rather than those divine things which are immortal, eternal, and universal. As a result, we are continually subject to disappointment and suffering, because our illusion may be shattered at any moment. The Buddha provided the antidote to this problem in his four noble truths and his eight-fold path for release from suffering. The eight-fold path is right attention, right thought, right attitude, right work, right intention, right speech, right meditation, and right remembrance.

The esoteric value of Buddhism is that it encourages us to harmonize ourself with the light of God so that we think, feel, speak, and act in ways which keep us attuned to God. The spiritual way of living, in other words, is not just a way of finding union with the divine but also a way to redeem the sorrows of life on earth.

Judaism. The Old Testament prophets, important to Judaism and Christianity alike, reveal numerous aspects of divine intelligence, divine order, and divine love. The lives of the prophets underscore the immense struggle of the spiritual aspirant against the forces of materialism and the deadly sins of greed, sloth, envy, vanity, anger, and arrogance. The record of the prophets also demonstrates how God uses qualified agents of light as vehicles for revealing His wisdom, law, and power.

In contrast to Hinduism, which reveals the impersonal nature of the universal God, Judaism reveals the dimension of God that is not only involved in our life but in fact quite concerned about it—so concerned that He frequently sends appointed messengers to help us find our way back to the Godhead.

The esoteric value of Judaism is primarily its emphasis on divine law. All of life is based on unvarying divine principles; the person who lives in harmony with these laws will be blessed by the love of God, but the person who mocks divine order will find that the law constantly exposes his misbehavior and selfishness. In contrast to the tendency of some people to view God in terms of sweetness and gentleness, Judaism makes it clear that God can be a "tough character" who disciplines those who rebel against Him. Unfortunately, the exoteric practices of the Jews have not preserved this esoteric message very well for the world. Instead of using divine law as a simple yardstick for their conduct, they took it as a license to generate a complex system of rules and regulations that all but drowns the original message in theocratic bureaucracy.

Perhaps the greatest esoteric contribution of the Jews is the Kabalah. The Kabalah is a complete alchemical system which combines a balanced approach to the power, law, intelligence, love, beauty, and order of God. It also gives us a means for understanding the various realms of creation which stand between the formless unity of the pure divine presence and the physical world as we know it. The worlds of forms, images, archetypes, and causes are all carefully depicted in the Kabalah, as well as the pathways or routes to the ten major aspects of God. As we learn to traverse the Kabalah as an inspired system of consciousness, we learn to move to and from the higher worlds. For the Western world, the Kabalah is an immense and rich body of knowledge about the inner side of life and how the invisible nature of God is related to all things visible.

Christianity. It is important to remember that Christianity is built on the base of established Judaism, just as Buddhism was built on the base of established Hinduism. In part, both the Buddha and the Christ came to add a new revelation of God's plan to the world, as well as to reform specific abuses of the religions of their day. Most of these reforms, happily, have been successful. Just as the Hinduism of today is far removed from that of the day of the Buddha, so also Judaism has progressed greatly in the last two thousand years.

The major esoteric contribution of the Christ was to present a fresh and profound revelation of the pervasive love of God. He taught and demonstrated that this divine power dwells within each of us. In addition, He stressed that this love should be expressed as charitable attitudes and acts toward our friends and neighbors—not just in devotion to God. Indeed, He taught that divine law could always be fulfilled by divine love, even when the literal meaning of the law might seem to be superseded. He did not reject the laws and teachings of the Old Testament prophets, but demonstrated through His own self-control, miracles, healings, and resurrection that divine love is more important than divine law. In essence, He liberated the West from the yoke of organized religion, as He taught that each of us is already important to God and can find God's nature and blessing through direct contact with the God within us. As a result, He has challenged all religions to stop relying on threats of guilt and fear to control people, but rediscover their true, esoteric purpose—which is to show the people the light within themselves.

Islam. The esoteric roots of Islam are basically the same as those of Christianity. The exoteric practices of Islam differ so greatly from those of Christianity that this fact may seem un-believable; nonetheless, it is true. Mohammed thought of himself as a disciple of the Christ and stressed the love of God and the need to demonstrate love just as the Christ had com-manded—to care for one another and to love God with all our heart, mind, soul, and might. The way this love has been demon-strated by Moslems in practice is often light years from what Mohammed originally intended, but this is just one more reason why we must look beyond the exoteric and discover the true esoteric heart of these systems.

Occult Traditions. Organized religion is often so absorbed in its own dogma that it is very difficult for true agents of light to work within existing systems. It is possible for astrologers to operate within the context of Hinduism, for instance, but inconceivable that they would be allowed to act with the blessing of most Christian churches. Even healing ministries find it difficult to take root and grow in most Christian fellowships, and healing was a practice constantly advocated and frequently demonstrated by the Christ! So, many legitimate esoteric traditions have had to develop outside of organized religion. Not surprisingly, they have been persecuted and condemned by the religiously fanatic as the work of the devil. But no system that helps us discover the presence of spirit can possibly be of the devil— although it is reasonable to think that the angry condemnations of the righteous *are* inspired by less than divine sources!

Together, these systems can loosely be labeled as "occult traditions." The word "occult" simply means "that which is hidden." Most of the major traditions in this division are as old or even older than the major religions. The fact that they have been preserved and are as vital as ever tends to suggest that they do not need the blessing of organized religion to serve their purpose. The blessing of God is sufficient. The major occult traditions include:

The Tarot. Ostensibly, the Tarot is a deck of cards from which our modern deck of playing cards descended. Originally, however, it was created as a way of translating complex esoteric ideas into a symbolic form that could be studied and gradually comprehended, regardless of cultural and educational differences. Each card in the major arcana represents a specific power, quality, or attribute of divine life. Each card in the minor arcana portrays a step in the physical, emotional, mental, and spiritual growth of the aspirant.

Over the years, the Tarot has been cheapened by use in fortune telling. This has created an exoteric tradition which not only colors and distorts most books written on the subject, but also subtly affects the intuitive perceptions of many people who use it. In using the Tarot, therefore, it is important to pierce through the astral thought-forms associated with its exoteric form, and work directly with the divine archetypes which originally inspired it.

Used in this way, the esoteric value of the Tarot is that it can help us understand the flow of power and intelligence from heaven to earth, and the steps we must take to become more skillful in managing these divine energies. Repeated use of the Tarot slowly builds a system of intelligence and association in our subconscious mind that becomes increasingly responsive to the direct inspiration of the divine archetypes.

Incidentally, the major arcana of the Tarot bears strong parallels to the Kabalah. Both of these traditions are carefully designed to give us a way to work directly with divine archetypes. As a result, they free us from having to depend upon faith and conformity to a sanctioned religion for our contact with God.

Astrology. It is amazing that so many Westerners see no logical contradiction in stating that God is omniscient while simultaneously claiming that astrology is bunk. Either they do not understand the nature of universal intelligence or the true workings of astrology—or both. Nevertheless, disbelief has never once affected the workings of divine intelligence. Life is pervaded by the wisdom of God, and everything in creation is affected by it. The same intelligence that guides the solar systems, the constellations, and the galaxies likewise shapes our character, consciousness, and opportunities to grow. Astrology is an ages-old system that uses the visible record of the heavens to reveal to us the invisible influences affecting our lives, individually and collectively.

It is no secret that the common practice of astrology bears little resemblance to its esoteric purposes. The emphasis of exoteric astrology on fatalism is repulsive. Still, the distortions that have occurred in astrology are probably fewer than can be found in any major religion. The esoteric value of astrology is that it provides us with an invaluable source of insight into human character and psychology. In addition, as we get into the advanced study of astrology, it reveals to us the incredible precision with which divine intelligence works. Properly pursued, the study of astrology can also teach us a system of hierarchical thought which becomes more and more useful as we grow in awareness and spiritual skill.

I Ching. The Chinese Book of Changes, or I Ching, is one of the greatest demonstrations of the principle of duality in action to be found anywhere in the world. The system is comprised of sixty-four hexagrams, symbols consisting of six horizontal lines stacked vertically. Each line is either solid or broken. Each of the sixty-four hexagrams represents a divine archetype, and each hexagram is also capable of changing into any other hexagram. In this way, the *movement* of divine forces, their evolution, and their impact on human awareness can be plotted, studied, and understood.

In China, the I Ching is revered as a system of philosophy which can be actively used to make sense of daily life. The study of it has drawn the attention of some of the most brilliant scholars in China's history. As a result, this is one esoteric tradition which has remained more or less esoteric, even though used for divination.

The esoteric value of the I Ching is that it reveals the inner forces of momentum—the hidden causes and influences—which guide and direct the outer circumstances of life.

Alchemy. This is an esoteric tradition which has faded in importance in the present day, due to our preoccupation with its exoteric counterparts. Yet it will inevitably arise once again in prominence, for the wisdom it contains is without equal. Carl Jung considered alchemy the precursor of modern psychology and saw in the ancient quest for the Philosopher's Stone a complete allegory to the psychological dynamism of the human being. Other parallels could be drawn as well, but the point is clear: the study of alchemy reveals to us the hidden drama of transformation, whether in the human, in chemical reactions, in nature, or in the heavens.

The stated purpose of alchemy is to discover a way to make gold out of base metals. Taken literally, this quest became an absurd exoteric waste of time. But taken symbolically, alchemy opens the aspirant to an intelligent, orderly system of transformation in which the base elements of the human system are purified and eventually transmuted into refined, noble elements capable of responding to the gold of spirit.

Cultural Traditions. At times, the best place to hide something is in plain sight of everyone. In much the same way, some of the most profound esoteric traditions are in plain sight of everyone, hidden within the exoteric trappings of a cultural tradition. These are customs and activities which can be pursued without any awareness of the inner life at all—but once the esoteric key is added, they take on a whole new meaning and importance. They then become as much a source of revelation about God and His plan as any religious or occult tradition. The major traditions of this type include:

Mythology. The myths of ancient cultures are often a profoundly rich source of esoteric revelation. In many cases, of course, the myths we record today of Egypt, Greece, Rome, and the Nordic and Germanic countries are the residues of the religions of ancient civilizations. The great religions have always used stories, fables, parables, and metaphors to educate people about God and God's plan for them. While many modern people would sniff haughtily at the thought of learning anything from pagan traditions, it is nonetheless true that the ancients were quite sophisticated in portraying the many different aspects of God's life, will, power, beauty, love, light, law, and harmony as various gods and goddesses.

In truth, many of the ancient myths are just as effective today as they were in ancient times, something that has been proven repeatedly since we updated the myth of the Muses, as a source of creative insight, and the myth of the Graces, as a source of inspired human behavior (see *The Art of Living,* volumes IV and V).

Not all myths are the residue of ancient religions, of course. The most powerful myth in the English culture is the story of King Arthur, the king who first united England. This tale began as an epic poem sung by Myrddin, who eventually evolved into the magician Merlin. Over the centuries, other elements were added. In its present form, it is a powerful story of spiritual transformation and the search for the Holy Grail.

Ultimately, all of literature should serve the same purpose as myths—and at its highest achievement, it does. Certainly some of our greatest poets have played their part in the esoteric tradition, whether it is William Shakespeare, Alexander Pope, or Ralph Waldo Emerson. In our modern day, the torch has been passed to our better writers of science fiction and fantasy. The writings of Robert Heinlein, Colin Wilson, Charles Williams, Talbot Mundy, Joan Grant, Dave Duncan, and Jack Chalker are laden with esoteric gold, waiting to be mined by the perceptive reader.

Masonry. Only the exoteric shell of freemasonry now remains, but not too many centuries ago it was a powerful source of esoteric instruction. The lessons required to pass initiation were similar to the beginning stages of the spiritual path, and the sense of ethics expected of every mason helped shape the character of many people. The fact that masonry has now degenerated into little more than a social club does not tarnish its esoteric roots.

The basic symbolism of masonry as a group of individuals coming together to build the city of God, brick by brick, through their own personal achievements, still remains as one of the great inspirations of spiritual growth.

The Path of the Hearthfire. One of the most ordinary of human activities is that of parenting and family care. But this ordinary role can take on mythological dimensions when the parents see the part they play as being enlightened guardians of their children and a divine companion for their spouse. When this change in emphasis occurs, then family life becomes what Dion Fortune referred to as "the path of the hearthfire."

Few activities can teach us more about the true nature of divine love than the commitment to cherish and nurture our family. The esoteric elements of family life are threefold:

1. Marriage. By wedding, we are given the opportunity to demonstrate the strength of our commitment, our willingness to subordinate personal desires to the needs of the partnership, and our ability to cherish, nurture, and care for another human being, both in good and bad times. These are all qualities which must be developed before we can establish a mature bond with the soul.

2. Birth. Physical birth is a natural process, but it quietly teaches even the densest materialist the lessons of spiritual birth. For with the birth of a child, the parents, too, are born. Consciously or unconsciously, they are taking on responsibility for this new life, pledging to care for it once it is born and nurture it and help it grow to adulthood. The drama of physical birth reveals to us, esoterically, the complete cycle for bringing any kind of new life into reality physically, be it a creative project, a new business, or a new movement in human evolution. As with physical birth, all human creation involves an initial impregna-

tion with the impulse to act, followed by commitment, a period of incubation, the birthing of our new ideas and plans, and finally, celebration of the achievement.

3. Death. The mundane response to death is grief, fear, and a sense of loss. Once we break through the bonds of the mundane, however, and grasp the esoteric meaning of death, we will replace our sense of grief with joy, our fear with beauty, and our sense of loss with a measure of fulfillment. For death is really the soul's celebration of the completion of another creative cycle. It marks the rebirth of our individuality into a new and higher level of life. It should therefore be viewed as a vital part of the process of transcendence, rather than a mystery shrouded in darkness and grimness.

By aspiring to an esoteric perspective on life as we deal with these three ordinary aspects of family life, we can transform the ordinary and the mundane into the spiritual and the enlightened.

The care of pets. The majority of people have pets for highly personal reasons—for example, to take the place of children a couple could never have, or to help children learn basic lessons of responsibility and affection. But esoterically, the care of pets takes on a special role in humanity's responsibility to act as steward for all life forms on this planet. By taking the more evolved forms of animals into our homes and lives and treating them as pets, we help accelerate their own evolution. These animals are "saved" from their instinctive habits and their natural life as hunters or wild beasts. Cats learn to coexist with other cats and natural enemies; dogs and horses learn to respond to commands and instructions of their human companions. In this way, we learn the basic lessons of being an agent of salvation, and help our favorite animals take a major step toward individuality.

Indeed, when the care of pets is filled with affection and joy, it becomes a way that many people fulfill the plan of God, without even realizing it.

Nature mysticism. In our modern life of shopping centers and jet travel, most of us must make a conscious effort to "return to nature" and learn the lessons it can teach us. But until just a few decades ago, most people did live in the midst of nature, and nature often taught them more about the inner life of God than trainloads of evangelists. For those who make the effort, nature mysticism can still be a powerful tool for revealing the life of spirit. It is hard for anyone but the densest materialist to spend more than five minutes in the midst of nature without realizing that all of life is filled with the beauty and love of God. Through an ongoing interaction with nature, we come to respect and comprehend something of the inner life, order, harmony, abundance, and benevolence of nature. We may even go beyond this level to recognize that we are part of this natural order and life and are sustained by it, even as our Father sustains the life of every sparrow.

A study of the life of American Indians before 1850 reveals that their knowledge of nature included far more than just ordinary lore. They were filled with a quiet reverence for the fact that they were part of the larger life and intelligence of earth.

One facet of nature mysticism deserves special mention—the tradition of the "little people" or "wee folk," the fairies, elves, gnomes, and leprechauns of folklore and fiction. These creatures are quite real and a necessary part of the life of nature. They are part of a vast, invisible support system for plant and animal life. They guide the growth of all forms of nature and link them to the great orders of angels who breathe life into all living forms on earth. People who come to love and respect any aspect of nature may in time also become responsive to these elemental creatures. This kind of contact, when nurtured, can help lead us to a greater appreciation of the intelligence of God's life and the involvement of the angelic kingdom in sustaining life on earth.

This is not a complete list of all esoteric traditions, of course, but it does embrace the highlights. All of these esoteric traditions, when intelligently used, will help us recognize and accept that there is more to life than the material world that we see and touch. These traditions exist for our own benefit, individually and collectively. If we ignore them, we remain trapped in our ignorance. But if we learn to use them, they can help open channels for us to the worlds of spiritual light, love, and power.

At the very least, a study of these esoteric traditions should help us understand that there is indeed far more to both heaven and earth than we ever dreamed.

ACTIVATING THE TRADITIONS

It should be understood that a person can easily spend an entire lifetime studying the Kabalah or world mythology and accomplish absolutely nothing of importance. It is likewise possible to become a world-renowned authority on Hindu or Christian theology, and not penetrate to one degree the esoteric reality of these religions. Even though these systems do exist and are available for our study, there is no guarantee that studying them will help us activate the inner light, love, and power associated with them. In many cases, in fact, we may just end up trapped in our own theories and concepts.

The spiritual seeker must learn to sidestep the many empty shells of popular dogma associated with most of these traditions and penetrate to the heart of the tradition. He must learn to identify intuitively with the esoteric forces which are the origins of the tradition, and move with them as they interact at an archetypal level. But there are any number of obstacles which will block his progress, if he allows it. These are the primary obstacles to be on guard against:

1. All of the genuine esoteric traditions are better known by their exoteric reputation. The Tarot, for instance, is best known as a device for fortune telling, not as a key to divine intelligence. The popular use of the Tarot tends to put us in touch with our subconscious wishes and desires, not the archetypal forces of divine life and destiny. In order to learn to use the Tarot effectively, we must be able to work without interference from our wishes and desires, which would otherwise drag us back down into its exoteric expression. In exactly the same way, in order to work effectively with the principles of Christianity, we must rise above the dogma and divisiveness of the established church and touch the heart of goodwill and peace that the Christ embodied.

2. The bias of organized religion that it is the one true way to God. The average person tends to assume that "religion" and "spiritual work" are one and the same, as if the only way God enters our life is through organized religion. This problem is compounded by the tendency of the righteous elements of

religion to view any competition with spiteful condemnation. It is, for instance, very common for fundamentalists to label other religions as well as the various occult traditions as "the work of the devil" or "abominations to the Lord." These people also dismiss mythology as the pagan creations of ignorant and superstitious cultures. Even if we do not personally believe in this bias, it can subtly affect our efforts. Many fine people are afraid to try to discover the higher self and the inner dimensions of divine life on their own, because they have been brought up in a culture that forbids it.

The truth is that the presence of God is revealed by every facet of life, if we have cultivated the eyes to see it. God did not create the world thousands of years ago and then depart. The Creator is present in everything that has life, as the sustaining force and directing intelligence behind the outer form. It should be the business of religion to point this out to us and encourage us to find every possible pathway to God.

3. The fear of the unknown. Any study of the esoteric requires a willingness to leave behind the known and venture into what is, as yet, unknown to us. This is often a threatening prospect to the personality, which is largely the product of our physical experiences. We are reluctant to take risks—even risks which might bring a huge payoff. We are content in most cases to stick with what we know, and let someone else take the lead in penetrating the unknown. The average person is therefore quite content to worship a tame and undemanding God who expects nothing more of us than our belief and unquestioning obedience. Yet teachings such as the parable of the talents make it clear that God does not want us to be a bunch of sheep. The divine plan calls for us to venture forth and taste of life, and in the process seize our divine birthright, our divine inheritance *to know*. But we cannot fulfill this aspect of the plan unless we have the courage and individuality to think for ourself, boldly explore the inner as well as the outer realms of life, and draw our own conclusions about what we believe in and stand for.

4. The intellectual inability to comprehend divine forces and qualities. The essence of any esoteric system is a set of abstract divine qualities and forces—a fragment of the divine plan, as it were. We are not used to working with abstract thought. Our

educational system trains us to think intellectually, but not intuitively. As a result, we usually lack the fundamental ability to interact abstractly with these esoteric forces. This problem is illustrated in the difficulty we have in studying flowers. We can take a rose and smell it, feel it, photograph it, draw it, and even taste it. But these sensations only tell us about the *appearance* of the rose. They reveal nothing about the *life essence* of the rose— the inner intelligence, purpose, vitality, and joy of the rose. This life essence is abstract, archetypal. It cannot be known intellectually, through physical observation. It can only be known by intuitive identification. The same is true of esoteric systems.

There are those who would scoff at this idea, claiming that it is irrelevant to attempt to understand God or any facet of His life. All we need to do, they say, is love Him and believe in Him. But these people are caught in the vicious circle of their own prejudices. God's intelligence pervades all of life, including us. We have been given the precious gift of consciousness so that we can become aware of this plan, understand it, and apply it to our own life. To do this, we must learn to think! We must develop a capacity for abstract realization. We must learn to penetrate through the appearance of ideas and harness the meaning and power at their core. Thinking involves a great deal more than memorizing dogma and collecting the theories of others; it requires us to interact with abstract concepts, philosophical principles, ethical precepts, and archetypal forces at *their own level.*

Even though many people are not mentally prepared to work effectively with esoteric ideas and traditions, the good news is that they can learn. And they must learn, because until they do, they will be as handicapped as a blind person visiting an art gallery. The blind person can touch sculptures and perhaps even the texture of an oil painting, but he will miss most of the subtle forms, shades, and colors the artist used to convey his inspiration. Just so, the untutored mind will miss most of what an esoteric tradition reveals.

These four obstacles to the correct activating of esoteric traditions can spawn a variety of problems which further obscure the issue. The most conspicuous of these problems are found in organized religion. The righteous are quick to adopt a proprietary interest in God. They cloak themselves with self-assumed authority and begin spewing forth all kinds of rules, prohibitions, and rituals. While they may begin with something abstract and spiritual, they quickly convert it into something as mundane as the rules for bowling. By trying to squeeze the abstract into a neat box of rules and rituals, they cripple the esoteric spirit which first inspired them. Thereafter, the rules and rituals are worshipped far more than the love or light of God. The Status Quo of organized religion has been created in the minds and hearts of the worshippers, and is fiercely defended ever after as "God on earth."

But heaven is not brought to earth by degrading it! The rituals of a religion have value—but only if they lead us back to their esoteric origins. A priest or minister who leads a communion service without any idea of the angelic and divine forces being summoned, or an inability to share that experience with the congregation, ought to give up the ministry and go into something he or she understands. A priest or minister who refuses to marry a young couple because they have not followed the rules of their religion ought to remember what Christ taught us—that divine love is stronger and more powerful than church rules. The church's function is to evoke a greater expression of spirit from each of us. Whenever its rules serve only to stifle the emergence of spirit, they should be cast aside.

But it is not just clerical malfeasance which weakens our esoteric traditions. Culture itself contributes to this process, by building up a group mind connected with each major esoteric system. Fed by the fear of the unknown and our difficulty in grasping abstract ideas, those who cherish the esoteric usually end up generating a body of uninspired and unimaginative thought about it. While this is inevitable to some extent, the danger is that we tend to substitute simplistic explanations for the essential truths of these esoteric traditions. This process slowly smothers the esoteric life within them, replacing it with theories and concepts more compatible with ordinary human thinking and prejudices. The easy comfort of the ordinary kills the esoteric life.

We can find many examples of this process in the Christian tradition alone. Spiritual love becomes translated into "feeling good about God" instead of acting in generous and helpful ways.

Charity is redefined in terms of giving money to the church, rather than treating our fellow human beings with a generous heart and mind. Confession to God becomes an exercise in berating ourself for our failures, rather than an act of renewing our faith and commitment to God. In these ways, centuries of pious followers can subtly distort and weaken the real message of any esoteric tradition, without anyone even realizing it. The challenge of pursuing excellence is blunted. The mystery of life is exchanged for comforting platitudes. The love of God gets reduced to the lowest human feeling. The wisdom of God becomes a collection of clichés. And this can have a profound impact on basic Christian teachings. Modern Christianity, for example, puts far more emphasis on the suffering and death of Jesus than on His life and resurrection. It is commonly assumed that Jesus died for our sins. As a result, many good people have concluded erroneously that suffering is a virtue by itself. And yet, these assumptions miss the obvious fact that Jesus served mankind by *living,* not by dying! He revealed the nature of God and the life of spirit by demonstrating God's grace and wisdom in His healings and miracles, and by transcending all things of earth—even the death of His physical body. *His intention was not to be remembered for dying–but because He did not die!*

Other esoteric traditions have suffered similar distortions. In the common uses of the Tarot, for instance, it is held that the suit of pentacles stands for physical wealth and success, whereas esoterically it represents *all* material issues and the grounding of spiritual and psychological forces through physical expression. In exoteric astrology, the influence of Scorpio is thought to make people sexy, manipulative, and cynical, whereas the esoteric meaning of this energy is that it tests us in the principal areas of our growth, so that we can see clearly where we need to grow, and what we have accomplished. In the usual interpretation of Greek mythology, the gods and goddesses are thought to portray human struggles and weaknesses, whereas the esoteric meaning of these stories actually reveals divine principles and the way life seeks to teach us.

To work with these esoteric traditions, therefore, we must be prepared to do battle with cultural prejudices and distortions, as well as our personal biases. We must prepare the mind to penetrate beyond the shallow, the superficial, and the obvious, and deal with reality as it is. Once again, we must rely on the principles for intelligent study that were postulated in the first essay in this book. These five principles are:

1. We must search always for *the multidimensional meaning* of these traditions. The physical record or experience of any system is the least meaningful, whether it is Christianity, the I Ching, or our relationship with pets.

2. We must try to discern *the inner life in which this tradition exists.* Since the inner life of all religions is brotherhood, for example, then bigotry has no place in religious expression. We should view all religious beliefs as part of a greater Whole.

3. We must look for and understand *the hierarchical structure* of laws, archetypes, purpose, and wisdom which governs a given system. No one on earth can assume authority for our spiritual growth. This is an authority that can be claimed only by the spirit within us. We should therefore use these esoteric traditions to help us grow and become an agent of light, not intimidate us.

4. We must learn to recognize *the universality* of these systems. The I Ching was developed in China, but works marvelously well in the West as well.

5. We must identify the elements of these systems that are *immortal and continuous.* The reputation of astrology may have suffered from the way it is currently practiced, yet the esoteric truths of astrology remain as vital and relevant today as they were ten thousand years ago.

Armed with these five guidelines and an active mind, we should be able to penetrate the miasmas of mundane traditions born of the confusion of century after century of misinterpretation of these systems. Whenever we find ourself becoming confused, we should take a step back and review the five principles, to make sure we are using them correctly.

A good example of the value of this approach can be found in interpreting the Tarot card "Death." The standard interpretations of this card are uniformly negative, threatening, and ominous. But once we penetrate through the fear and anxiety surrounding this card, we find that death is just another archetypal force. Death is not anything to fear; on the contrary, it is a spiritual quality we need to learn to use constructively in our life—to bring a specific cycle of growth or achievement to an end, so we can move on to new challenges. We need to be able to use death to eliminate bad habits, immature attitudes, and ignorant beliefs. Indeed, as we rise above the standard interpretations of death, we find that it inevitably leads to rebirth—a rebirth into *the higher dimensions* of spiritual wisdom, love, and power within us. Death, in other words, can release something of *the larger life* of spirit within us, and at the same time, reveal to us *the higher order* of forces, wisdom, and love that has always guided us. The proper study of death also reminds us of the *constancy* of change in our life. Death is painful only if we try to cling to that which we are leaving behind. Yet behind this continual change we can glimpse the *universal* nature of spirit and the working of divine purpose and law.

Acting in this way, we can investigate any esoteric tradition to discover the spiritual elements within it, and what it means to act as a spiritual agent of its power. We do not have to join a group to learn these lessons; we can undertake it as an independent course of study, freeing us from the limitations of teachers, books, and man-made rules. We can learn from our own inner potential for wisdom.

There is an old saying that the careful study of anything ultimately leads us to God. In this case, "careful" means that we proceed in a hierarchical manner. We begin with an exoteric teaching and examine it for meaning. First, we try to understand it in the context it is usually taught. Eventually, however, this effort will lead to certain paradoxes and areas of confusion; we end up with more questions than we started with. Taking these questions, we then begin to look at the teaching multidimensionally. We search for the inner meanings of the outer phenomena. We try to ascertain the greater life in which the exoteric teaching has its being and significance. We postulate the hierarchical structure of laws, causes, purposes, and priorities which give this system order. We seek out evidence of the system's universality and renewability.

In actual application, this means we can start with any esoteric tradition and end up discovering God. We might select the Arthurian myth, the story of Jonah, a Sufi story, or an I Ching hexagram for our investigation; it does not matter, for the procedure is the same. For the sake of illustration, let us consider the myth of Hercules. Exoterically, this myth is just an entertaining story—an ancient soap opera. In truth, however, the myth of Hercules is a set of stories about the tests and trials a spiritual aspirant must endure as he proves his merit. Hercules is given twelve labors to perform; each represents the achievement of a certain stage of mastery in the use of our mind, emotions, and will.

The eleventh labor, for example, is the cleaning of the Augean stables. These stables had not been cleaned in thirty years; the result was widespread pestilence and blight within the stables and the surrounding area. Instead of physically removing the dung, Hercules decided to break down the walls of the stables. Then he diverted the flow of two local streams into the stables. As the water flowed through them, the stables were washed clean. While this action neatly accomplished the task at hand, the king who had given Hercules the task was disappointed; he considered it some kind of trick rather than a genuine accomplishment of Hercules himself.

To understand the esoteric meanings of this tale, we must look beyond the literal adventure. It is easy to recognize that Hercules took a creative and independent course of action. But what do the years of accumulated refuse in the stables stand for? The pestilence? What archetypal realities do these conditions represent? What forces led up to such an accumulation of toxins? What aspect of spirit does Hercules embody? And what is the esoteric relevance of breaking down the walls of the stable and redirecting the rivers?

As we reflect on these questions, we begin to discover the answers. The thirty years of accumulated animal refuse stands for the uncleansed state of our mind, emotions, habits, and memories, which slowly drags us down into fear, doubt, worry, resentment, and apathy, unless we clean them up regularly. These are the psychological toxins which can poison us and everything around us.

The story teaches us that we are in jeopardy if we stand still, clinging to the status quo, expecting others to rescue us from our own folly or laziness. Help from friends and spiritual quarters may be close at hand, but closed off to us, as long as we wait passively, believing, hoping, and expecting miracles to save us. We must save the situation instead by taking intelligent and forceful action. Hercules stands for the principle of active intelligence in our character, the strong man who looks for innovative and effective solutions and then carries them out.

Hercules breaks down the walls of the stables so that the toxins can be swept out by the force of the two rivers. The walls symbolize the structure of our habits and beliefs that isolate and alienate us from one another and the life of spirit. The bricks of these walls are our own arrogance, selfishness, self-deception, greed, apathy, and ignorance. We have to be a strong man or woman indeed to take the action which will eliminate these barriers.

In the end, Hercules achieves success, but the king thinks it has been some kind of trick. This turn of events symbolizes the fact that wise actions are often misunderstood and even rejected by ordinary human opinion and authority. We must therefore be guided by our inner, divine wisdom—not the standards of the rest of the world.

None of these insights will come to us, of course, unless we ask intelligent questions about the meaning of the story, look for the symbolic relevance of the characters and events, and inquire what all this means to our present situation. We must look for the presence of spiritual law, purpose, and intelligence at work in whatever tradition we may be studying. Then we must relate these insights to our own situation and ask ourself if there is a message in it for us. Are there things that we, and only we, can do to help ourself? Is there something we must do or stop doing to attain a greater harmony with the life of spirit? Are we too bound by tradition or the need for external advice and approval to realize spiritual solutions for our life? Thinking and speculating in this way is what opens the doors to the real power of these esoteric systems.

But this is just half of the story of harnessing esoteric traditions. Understanding must always come first, but once understanding has arrived, it must then be activated for practical activity. In other words, we must harness the spiritual force the tradition has revealed to us, and begin expressing it in our life.

Let us assume that we have just finished reading about the

Buddha or the Christ and have been struck by the tremendous peace and patience each of them exhibited. Is it enough to understand that they tapped the archetypal force of peace and constantly expressed it in their lives? Is it enough just to admire these great examples, satisfied that we completely understand the need for this virtue? Of course not. The lesson is meaningless until we learn to harness the power of divine peace and patience and express it in our own life.

So we need to ask ourself: what is peace? Is it just a nice, comfortable feeling? Is it a state of being quiet and withdrawn? What does it mean to be patient at the mental level? What is the nature of the archetypal force behind patience? What is the impact of this force on us? What changes must we make within ourself to be able to express and sustain peace and patience in our life? How can we apply these qualities in the midst of a busy daily life?

As we learn about patience, we will find that it is an expression of the divine quality of peace. This force is an active, dynamic power; it induces greater activity, not rest or relaxation. The greatest expression of peace, therefore, is the ability to stay calm and inner directed even in the midst of opposition, chaos, and turmoil. It is the ability to stand at the mountain top, master of all we survey, in charge of self and our behavior, as well as the forces swirling all around us. Patience is the ability to proceed in harmony with the ideal divine rhythm behind any activity, acting when we should, but refraining from acting when the time is not right.

Insight gives us the vision of what we must attain. But attaining it is a long process of practice, correction, and renewed practice. It is the journey of the spiritual path. And whether our goal is peace or any other quality of the divine life, we need to know where the journey begins and where it ends. This is the work of the esoteric traditions—to show us the way.

Eventually, as we come to understand and express these inner qualities, through repeated work in any given esoteric tradition, a most wonderful thing happens. We create within our consciousness a structure of thought, force, and divine light which is a miniature version of the esoteric tradition in its own right. In other words, after years of properly using the Tarot, we build into our own consciousness a miniature version of the Tarot. The archetypal forces which live in the Tarot come to life in our own awareness. Just the same, after years of working intelligently with the Buddha's eightfold noble path, we may well find the noble path within ourself. This is a sure sign that we are properly activating the spiritual essence of the tradition.

SERVING THE LIGHT

It is not always easy to live up to the challenges of becoming an agent of these esoteric traditions. It is all too easy to look around us, see friends and colleagues who never even think esoterically, and decide that our knowledge is enough; we do not have to actually act on it all the time. It is easy—but also disastrous. As we work with these esoteric traditions, they take root in our consciousness. It is important to work with them steadily, faithfully, and nurture their growth within our own development.

In doing this, we can be inspired by the example of all the enlightened people known to history. The true teachers of mankind never preach one thing and then act in another way. They reveal the presence of God within the acts of their own lives. Their teachings are secondary; it is what they do that counts primarily.

The Buddha, for instance, demonstrated the compassionate understanding of suffering and the way to transcend it. The great Hindu sages demonstrated transcendence over things of the earth. The great teachers of the Tao demonstrated how to live a spiritual life "in the marketplace" of active, human affairs—as opposed to an ashram or monastery. The great Jewish prophets embodied the force of divine law and demonstrated its power in their struggles with the forces of materialism and egotism. The Christ embodied the principle of divine love, demonstrating the fullness of the divine potential within each of us, as well as the power of divine love.

Unfortunately, the great teachers of God's light and love are not usually on tap for a personal consultation. And it is extremely uncommon nowadays for angels to appear and instruct us. Pillars of fire and burning bushes have not been reported for thousands of years. And so, we must make do with the example of these great teachers as we seek to unravel the mysteries of the esoteric traditions. We must internalize their examples and discover the methods by which they first learned them. We must learn to think. And as we learn, we must break down the barriers of ignorance and arrogance within us that have shut out the light of our soul.

We must find our own revelation of God through direct experience. We cannot let a minister or theologian or expert do it for us. We can profit from excellent examples, but we must do the work. The esoteric traditions show us the way, but it is up to us to set forth on the journey—and keep with it until we reach our goal.

As the Christ admonished us: "No one lights a lamp to put it under a tub; they put it on the lampstand where it shines for everyone in the house. In the same way your light must shine in the sight of men, so that, seeing your good works, they may give the praise to your Father in heaven."

The only obstacles that stop us from letting our light shine are of our own making. Just as the Pharisees were trapped by the letter of the law, we can be trapped by truth concepts and stale platitudes. We may even understand, yet still fail to act. But the true life of wisdom inspires us to rise above these limitations—the limitations of theories and dogma, and our personal failures to act responsibly.

Wisdom frees us from all obstacles!

The Inner Teachings
Of the Bible

The Bible is not just a story of spiritual happenings from two thousand years ago—it is an ageless account of the spiritual life. Properly used, it is a guide to tapping the spiritual resources of divine wisdom, love, and action. This essay shows us how to harness the light of the inner teachings of the Bible for our spiritual enrichment.

THE LIVING PRESENCE OF GOD

Every human culture develops sacred traditions and writings. This is as true for the American Indians as it is for the Buddhists of Asia, the Moslems and Jews in the Middle East, and the many Christian sects and religions throughout the world. In more primitive societies, these scriptures begin as oral traditions and legends which are eventually translated into written words. In more educated societies, the sacred writings generally consist of the letters and papers of great enlightened teachers and their closest disciples. Sometimes, even the commentaries of theologians or spiritual philosophers on the meaning of the existing traditions are included as part of the sacred literature of the society.

Collectively, these sacred writings comprise a rich repository of important ideas concerning the nature of God and how we can establish a closer relationship with our Creator. They help shape the values and character of the society in which they developed. As such, they should be regarded as a great treasure—as well as an important revelation about life.

In the West, the major sacred text is the Bible. It contains all of the three principal kinds of sacred teaching: the insights and revelations of major prophets, commentaries by their closest disciples and associates, and revered oral traditions which were handed from one generation to the next until they were finally set down in print. The Bible is nothing less than an astounding volume of profound revelations about the nature of God and our potential as children of God to live a full and inspired life.

Nonetheless, as majestic as the Bible is, it must be recognized that it is not the final word or even the only word on Judeo-Christian thought and spiritual teaching. For one thing, it is not especially well organized. Many portions are difficult to comprehend. In places, the Bible can be a confusing book, full of contradictions, obscure allegories, and esoteric mysteries. The teachings presented are just as often obtuse as they are lucid. At times, there can be a maddening lack of detail, forcing us to fill in the dots. In addition, there is an obvious provincial bias in many of the books of the Old Testament.

Compounding these problems is a second grave limitation. Most everyone would agree that the Bible—as well as other scriptures like it—is an extremely important guide to the life of spirit. But some people seriously overstate its value, to the point where they idolize the *form* of the Bible. By a leap of faith not endorsed or supported by the Bible itself, these people declare it to be the literal word of God, inerrant and perfect. They devote their time not to understanding the meaning of the Bible and the inner realities it reveals, but to defending their closed-minded position that the Bible is the holy of all holies, the final, complete statement of God on every facet of life. This belief forces them into a trap of their own creation; because they are sure the Bible is the word of God, they are able to interpret it only in the most literal, simplistic ways. In some instances, this reduces their image of God to a meanspirited, capricious old goat—the kind of person or being no one would invite to a party or family gathering. God is not anything of the kind, of course, but this is what narrow-minded, fanatic thinking can do to the wisdom, love, and beauty of a great work like the Bible—if not restrained.

To understand the inner teachings of the Bible, therefore, we must approach it with an open mind. We must realize that any fanatically held belief about the Bible will seriously limit our ability to grasp the genuine wisdom to be found in this—or any—sacred text. If we truly want to be guided by the power and inspiration within the Bible, we must have the courage and wisdom to put aside any concept or belief that would obscure our comprehension of this great work.

To begin with, we must realize that the word of God is not something that can ever be written down. The word of God is the power and light of God—an abstract force that is both universal and invisible. It can have visible and tangible manifestations, but a manifestation of God or spirit is never the same as the true nature of God or spirit. At best, a manifestation will be a derivative of God's light and power—it can never be His full force and glory. This idea can perhaps best be understood by analogy. A loaf of bread can be a manifestation of the abundance of nature, but it can never be the full force and essence of abundance. Abundance is an abstract quality; a loaf of bread is a finite, tangible manifestation. This concept can also be conveyed in the notion that a map is not the same as the landscape it describes; nor is a picture of a mountain the same as the mountain itself. Metaphysicians would go a step further, and state that ideas expressed in written or spoken words can be a vehicle for the truth behind ideas, but never the wholeness or archetypal essence of truth. In other words, *it is impossible for written or spoken words to convey the fullness of divine truth.* They may convey a portion of truth, or point toward truth, but truth itself is the very energy of divine ideas and principles—invisible and universal.

The major concepts presented in the Bible *do* have their origin in the power and light of God. This is what makes the Bible sacred, and why reading the Bible is one of the best ways to exercise both our mind and our spiritual nature. But it is extremely dangerous to let respect and reverence for the divine origin of the Bible degenerate into a harmful idolization of the literal words and concepts. It distorts the meaning of the Bible in addition to degrading and cheapening the intelligence of the human mind. Such mindless idolatry is *not* part of the life of spirit.

Secondly, it is important to understand that the Bible is not just a codification of major Western teachings about the life of spirit. It is actually several different types of books all wrapped up in one volume. On one level, it is a historical document. On another, it is a treatise on philosophy and ethics. On a third, it is an esoteric text, full of allegory and symbolism about the inner life. There is even a fourth level; the Bible is a summons to each of us to respond to the life of spirit within us and everywhere around us.

Unfortunately, there is a fifth level, too—one that might be called the "shadow Bible." This level was not written into the Bible; it is the work of a group Jesus referred to as the "generation of vipers"—malicious, pompous people who gleefully excise statements from the Bible, restate them out of context, and then use them to justify their bigoted condemnations of mankind. In some cases these individuals do not even bother to quote the Bible; they just attribute their own words to Jesus or one of the prophets.

It is important to appreciate each of these levels within the Bible, both legitimate and illegitimate.

The most basic level of the Bible is that of a history of the Jewish nation and the early days of Christianity. If we accept this historical perspective, then we can begin to appreciate how profoundly the human race has evolved spiritually over the thousands of years represented by the Bible. We can understand that while certain injunctions were appropriate for ancient days—how to prepare animal sacrifices or care for one's concubines—they are completely out of harmony with modern needs and spiritual practices. The force of evolution has outmoded the literal words and concepts.

When the Bible is seen as a historical document, it is also much easier to make sense of many of its inconsistencies. There is, for example, a tremendous dichotomy between the jealous and vengeful image of God portrayed in the Old Testament and the loving, supportive image of God depicted by the Christ. The Psalms frequently invoke God's curse on the enemies of Israel—while Jesus commands us to love our enemies. If we assume that everything in the Bible is literally true, then the only conclusion we can draw from this contradiction is that God somehow underwent an enormous change in character between the time of David and the time of Jesus. This idea is so staggering that it could only be taken seriously by extremely arrogant people. On the other hand, if we accept the Bible as a historical document, we can see these discrepancies as evolutionary changes in humanity, not God. It was the Jewish tribe itself that changed between the times of David and Jesus—not God.

At the same time, however, it would not be quite accurate to limit the Bible to just being a history of the Jews and early Christians. It is much more than that: it is also the history of the evolution of the whole of humanity as we have struggled to understand how our human nature relates to our divine nature. The Bible is a record of the saga of human weakness and selfishness on the one hand, and of mankind's capacity for sacrifice, compassion, and creativity on the other. It is a report on our struggle to defeat the darkness in our lives and move toward the light of God. As such, it has a tremendous message for every individual, not just Jew or Christian.

The level most people interact with when they read the Bible is the aspect which sets forth the ethics and rules of spiritual living. As a text on spiritual philosophy, the Bible gives somewhat inconsistent advice, if the Old Testament is included with the New. Nonetheless, there is a wealth of ideas about how to deal with anger, fear, grief, despair, egotism, and the need to obey God—as well as harness the opportunities of success and abundance. In addition, there are brilliant commentaries on the correct way to pray, worship, contemplate, celebrate life, and meet misfortune. As a whole, the Bible as a spiritual guide is a singular statement on enlightened living.

The level of the Bible most commonly missed is that which reveals the inner side of human nature and the work of the spiritual path—*the esoteric Bible.* This esoteric side of the Bible is routinely ignored by those whose closed minds fail to rise above the literal words on the page. It is mocked by those who insist that the Bible is a book of prophecy about the impending doom we have induced through our "sinful ways." But even worse, the esoteric messages of the Bible are actually feared by those people who, having already carefully interpreted everything in the Bible to fit their world view, are terrified anyone might recognize more light in it than they do.

As an esoteric text, the Bible must be read as allegory and metaphor, not just as literal teachings and simple stories. The story of Adam and Eve in the Garden of Eden, for example, must be seen as something more complex than just a quaint myth about the origins of mankind and its "fall from grace." Eating the fruit of the tree of knowledge refers esoterically to how we separate ourself from God through our intense identification with the outer forms and appearances of life. In this sense, we figuratively eat of the apple every time we engage in malicious gossip, indulge in anger or grief, or otherwise pay too much attention to the false knowledge of the forms of life, rather than spirit.

Even historical events recorded in the Bible, such as the transfiguration or resurrection of Jesus, should be seen as having esoteric as well as historical relevance. As Jesus told us, whatever He did, we will eventually be able to do as well. The key events in His life are therefore instructions in basic spiritual truths and lessons that all of us must eventually learn and master. In fact, they reveal to us in symbolic form the nature of the spiritual path each aspirant must tread. To view them only as isolated experiences in the life history of a great prophet, unrelated to our individual life, represents a serious devaluation of their meaning.

No one should ever fear discussing the esoteric aspects of the Bible. The Bible was not written to be read by literal-minded people; it was written as a resource for spiritual contemplation. To derive full benefit from it, we must raise our consciousness to a spiritual level of reflection before reading any passage of the Bible. From this level, we will be able to recognize the hidden depths of insight and experience contained in the Bible—and how they apply to our life. No less an authority than Paul encouraged this approach in his first letter to the Corinthians 2:11: "It is only a person's own spirit within him that knows all about him; in the same way, only God's Spirit knows all about God....Whoever does not have the Spirit cannot receive the gifts that come from God's Spirit. Such a person really doesn't understand them; they are nonsense to him, because their value can be judged only on a spiritual basis. Whoever has the Spirit, however, is able to judge the value of everything, but no one is able to judge him."

It is therefore reasonable to view the Bible as a direct summons of the highest and noblest elements within each of us. As a book filled with guideposts and references to divine truth, it is difficult to pick it up and start reading it—even at random—without coming across a message which seems to have been written just for us. It was not written only for us, of course, but the Bible does have an enormous capacity to speak directly to our individual needs.

It is unfortunate that there is a highly vocal and forceful minority of zealots who "don't have the spirit" but who nonetheless declare themselves to be what H.L. Mencken termed "virtuosi of virtue." These self-styled experts are the militant moralists "who hold that all human acts must be either right or wrong and that 99.9999 percent of them are wrong; who believe that the right to forbid is invariably superior to the right to do...

connoisseurs of sin—in others." In the hands of these "connoisseurs of sin," the Bible loses its value as an esoteric revelation, a guide to spiritual and ethical living, and even much of its historical validity. It becomes just another tool for their blighted propaganda and malice.

The actual tone of the Bible is, of course, completely at odds with such heavy-handed righteousness. The fullness of the Bible reveals consistently that God is a benevolent, nurturing God who acts as our shepherd and also calls us to be shepherds of His life as well. He is powerful, yes, and embodies divine law—but both the power and law of God are fulfilled and implemented with benevolence and mercy. God is involved in our life and concerned about our long-term welfare and progress. In book after book in the Bible, we encounter a God who wants us to understand our nature, learn our lessons, reform our wayward ways, and accept the abundance of the spiritual life. God is depicted far more often as protective than as punitive, as caring than as condemning. But the connoisseurs of sin read a different message, one that is largely a product of the malice in their hearts and the "log in their eye," as Jesus put it.

The basic message of the Bible is not sin, but our liberation from whatever traps us. This may be sin—but it may also be narrowminded bigotry. Instead of being obsessed with sin, we should ponder on the words of Paul, this time from his second letter to the Corinthians (13:17-18): "Where the Spirit of the Lord is present, there is freedom. All of us, then, reflect the glory of the Lord with uncovered faces; and that same glory, coming from the Lord, who is Spirit, transforms us into his likeness in an ever greater degree of glory."

In this idea that all of us reflect the glory of the Lord lies the key to the intelligent use of the Bible. We have our problems, to be sure—even our tired, old retreaded sins. But when we open the Bible, we are challenged to go beyond our problems, beyond our sins. We are challenged to let the words of the Bible lead us beyond what we know about daily life and behold the power of divine truth, love, and strength. We are meant to fill ourself with these forces of spirit, and then find ways to translate them into our own character, work, and self-expression.

We are meant to discover the presence of divine intelligence in life—and realize that we are designed to use our own intelligence to serve this resource of spiritual wisdom.

We are meant to discover the presence of divine love in life—and comprehend that we have the capacity to refine our own goodwill, benevolence, and compassion so that we become an agent of God's love in our own life.

We are meant to discover the presence of divine strength in life—and become an active participant in the spiritual evolution of humanity.

It is not enough just to study the Bible for ideas. To activate it as a proper resource of spiritual living, we must use it as a dynamic vehicle for tapping divine wisdom, love, and strength. Then—and only then—does the Bible live up to its full potential as a path to the treasures and gifts of spirit.

THE UNDERLYING PRINCIPLE

The first great resource the Bible reveals to the perceptive spiritual aspirant is *divine intelligence.* God did not just dream up His creation capriciously; the whole of life is based on wise and intelligent patterns, laws, and principles. Because our human intelligence falls short of universal intelligence, we often fail to comprehend the wisdom of God. We focus on our problems, and begin to question if God knows what He is doing. We look at the disease and violence in life, and wonder if God is benevolent. But these are *our* shortcomings, not *God's.* Properly read and understood, the Bible can lead us beyond these shortcomings. It is a tremendous revelation of divine intelligence.

The key, of course, is learning to read the Bible properly. All too many people are not looking for wisdom when they read the Bible. They read it in an adversarial mood, seeking rules by which to judge others and divide what is right from what is wrong. They are looking for a justification to condemn their enemies in specific and human life in general, instead of seeking insight into how they can heal imperfection and serve the divine plan. They reduce divine intelligence to rules, regulations, and long lists of *shoulds, don'ts,* and *musts.*

We cannot tap the essence of divine intelligence by reducing it to a bunch of hard-and-fast rules, any more than we should ever believe that the essence of freedom is expressed through laws and governmental regulations. Freedom is a quality of life; laws can be designed to protect and encourage freedom, but the very same laws can also be used maliciously to limit and destroy freedom. To tap the essence of freedom, we must look beyond man-made laws. Just so, to tap the essence of divine intelligence, we must look beyond religious rules and rituals. We must see the Bible as an eloquent statement of *the fundamental spiritual principles of living.*

Jesus made this point repeatedly in His ministry. The Old Testament, for example, is filled with rules and laws defining the ritual of the Sabbath. These rules declared, among other things, that no work of any kind was permitted. Jesus, however, ignored this injunction and openly healed people on the Sabbath. In return, He was charged with violating the Sabbath's sanctity. He responded that the Sabbath—indeed, all of religion—was made for the people, not the other way around. He scolded the priests for making too much of rules and ritual and ignoring the *principle* of the Sabbath, which is to take time to remember and honor what is holy. Jesus healed by calling forth the presence of God in people—surely a legitimate way to remember and honor what is holy.

In spite of this remarkable demonstration of an underlying spiritual principle, and what it means to apply it, we still see the Sabbath abused today. Millions of "pious" people flock to church or temple and perform the rituals of their religion, but they are going more to see and be seen than to honor God and remember what is holy. The Sabbath has become a social exercise, not a religious remembrance.

Jesus challenged us repeatedly to go beyond ritual and rules and to think in the clear light of divine intelligence. In the Sermon on the Mount, He told us not to be obsessed with the clothes we wear, the food we eat, or the drink we need to slake our thirst. If God can take care of the birds and flowers when they do not work or make clothes for themselves, He said, then why should we doubt that God can take care of our needs? "Our life is worth more than food and the body is worth more than clothes," He declared. This advice is not a declaration that poverty is spiritual, that anorexia is admirable, or that we should dress like slobs, however. It is another statement of spiritual principle: that we need to focus our attention on the *quality* of our life—values, thoughts, and behavior—instead of being completely preoccupied with the outer appearances of life. We need to establish proper spiritual priorities, based on our understanding of the divine patterns of life.

In much the same spirit, Jesus told us that what we put into our mouth would never defile us as much as what came out of it. When He said this, He was being challenged for letting His disciples eat certain foods in violation of established rules of fasting and religious ceremony. There have always been food fanatics who make far too much of what we eat. Jesus was declaring an important spiritual principle for these people to hear: that what we say and how we act in general is far more important spiritually than what we eat. It is far more important to abstain from meanness than from meat, to forego whining than wine. He was also suggesting, in essence, that eating all the fresh vegetables in the county cannot make up for being dishonest or rude.

When we look for spiritual principles, rather than rules and restrictions, the Bible is filled with practical insights and guidance. It tells us, for instance, how to pray. Prayer in particular is often misused—to curse our enemies or to try to use divine forces to supply our material lusts. There is nothing wrong with wanting a new Mercedes, but praying for one is an abuse of prayer. Jesus advised us repeatedly to seek first (as highest priority) the kingdom of God—the qualities of love, joy, peace, gentleness, courage, wisdom, and patience within our spiritual self—and everything we need will come to us. This advice indicates a need to reassess our priorities and values so that they are in harmony with spiritual purpose. Then, when we pray, we are to ask for what God wants for us—*Thy will be done on earth as in heaven*—and for what we need—*Give us our daily bread*—not just what we, as a personality, may want. Even today, this is a spiritual principle that is commonly ignored, especially in those groups that have the arrogance to assume that God actually wants us all to drive a new Mercedes.

Effective prayer is a private communication with God. It must be approached quietly and humbly, not as a public exhibition of piety. Jesus warned against those who make a conspicuous display of public prayers in order to get attention and be hailed as ultraspiritual. He stated that God never has to answer such prayers, because these people have already received everything they actually wanted—attention and notoriety. Once again, it is the principle that counts—not the act.

Jesus likewise made it clear that worship is not something that is limited to one day of the week and the inside of a church or temple. Worship occurs whenever we bring our whole self to God; it can occur at work or in the supermarket as well as in a holy shrine. Nor does it require the correct enunciation of certain pious words or the proper sequence of sacred rituals, as though we were sending a semaphore message to God. *We worship God in how we live and what we do.* Jesus repeatedly told would-be disciples to sell all that they had, take up their cross, and follow Him. These words are not to be taken literally, of course—but we are meant to take the underlying spiritual principle seriously. We must give up our attachments to the things of the world and embrace our spiritual duties (the cross) in such a way that we reveal the presence of God within us. We must commit our talents, love, and life to God, not just through an occasional gift of time or money or perfect attendance at church, but by expressing God's life and love in everything we do. Formal religious services may well enhance this worship, but they are not a substitute for the real work of celebrating divine life.

The Bible likewise tells us that effective worship involves a constant alertness to the presence of God. We are to turn our attention toward God not just on the Sabbath, but at *all* times. Jesus repeatedly told parables about the need for servants to wait up for the return of the master, or of a bride waiting for the groom to arrive. These stories remind us that it is our spiritual duty to be constantly attentive to the presence of God—in nature, in the ways others treat us, in the opportunities that come to us, in the way divine justice works, and even in the lessons we learn. This is a full-time job. But unless we can find and honor God in the ordinary experiences of daily life, it may mean little to get a glimpse of Him occasionally during conventional worship services.

The insights to be found in the Bible are not limited to

helping us pray and worship more effectively, however. Many are quite practical. For example, there are many passages in the Bible advising us how to cultivate healthy, spiritual relationships with others. Jesus declared: "No more 'love your friends but hate your enemies!' Now I say that you must love your enemies, too." Unfortunately, this concept is almost as untried today as it was twenty centuries ago. There are legions of experts who believe that anger is a sign of strength and mental health. Yet Jesus made it clear that we cannot be angry and in harmony with God at the same time. If we go to worship bearing a grudge against a neighbor, He told us, we should leave and make peace with that neighbor before attempting to worship. If we are insulted, we should turn the other cheek. If we are exploited, we should go the "extra mile."

These admonitions strike many people as foolish and naïve—fit only for wimps and morons who do not know how to stand up for their rights. But these people obviously have never taken the time to reflect on the spiritual principles behind the words. If taken literally, it is true that these suggestions might turn some people into doormats for the pettiness and abuse of others. But these are not just empty words. Jesus was pointing out to us that the divine forces of tolerance and goodwill are far more important than an occasional embarrassment—or even exploitation. Hiding behind a wall of anger or aggressiveness estranges us from the divine nature within us—our birthright of goodwill and joy. No one's exploitation or manipulation of us is ever worth the price of giving up God's love and light. If we meet anger with anger, we double the anger—and lose the love of God we might otherwise express. But if we are centered in goodwill and wisdom, we will probably be able to find a way to deflect the dishonesty, rudeness, and brazen behavior of others with skill and courage, rather than anger, indignation, irritation, or retaliation. As long as we stay centered in the love of God, we retain the potential to heal the problem at hand. But once we give in to anger and intimidation, we get caught in an endless cycle of retribution.

To let anger and intolerance rule us is to let the "spirit of the earth" and the "law of the jungle" dominate us. The Bible teaches us a better way: to lift our sights and consciousness so that we can incorporate more of God's design and life into our daily behavior. Even when situations require a forceful display of authority and individuality, it can be done with dignity and fairness. But first, we must grasp the basic spiritual principle that we are meant to demonstrate the love and compassion of God not only in the way we treat other people—all people—but also in the way we approach the injustices, imperfections, and imbalances in our world and ourself.

These are just a few examples of how the Bible reveals the underlying principles of divine intelligence to us. The lesson to be learned is that we have not been left on our own, without a compass to guide us. The Bible is filled with helpful stories and examples that reveal to us the most intelligent and productive way to act in almost every life situation. To tap this resource, however, we must stop thinking of the Bible as a collection of rules and regulations, and start viewing it as an encyclopedia of the basic spiritual principles of living. We are meant to embrace these principles and learn to apply them creatively and meaningfully in our changing times and circumstances. At times, we may be criticized for breaking rules, just as Jesus was chastized. But if we understand the principle, we need not fear petty criticism. So long as we are revealing the presence of God within us, we can be sure we are acting intelligently.

LOVE IN ACTION

It is common knowledge that bureaucracies, whether in government, social agencies, or businesses, generally take care of themselves first and serve the public second. There are many glowing exceptions to this observation, of course, but corruption within the management of bureaucracies is an age-old problem.

This is as true in the bureaucracies of the major religions as it is in any other field. It is therefore not surprising that most official religions have usually worked diligently to promulgate rules and restrictions that increase their authority and prestige— by keeping the true nature of God and spirit hidden from the average person. In one way or another, it always seems that the clergy ends up "owning" God and proclaiming themselves to be the only authorized outlet for His message and blessings.

The basic trick in this spiritual sleight of hand is to make people dependent upon the clergy for access to God. The treatment of the sacrament of baptism is a good example of the clergy at work. In many cases, they have no compunction about claiming that baptism is an absolute necessity before God can enter a person's life; without baptism, God will be excluded forever and the individual will go straight to hell after dying. There is of course no Biblical support for these outlandish and absurd claims, but a lack of evidence has never been much of an impediment to the clergy.

No ritual performed by the clergy puts God into anyone. God puts Himself into every human being as part of the act of creating a new life. Baptism can be a meaningful celebration of the recognition of the presence of God within us—but it is not necessary to be baptized to live a spiritual life.

It should also be understood that the clergy has no power to expel us from the presence of God, either through excommunication or any of the more subtle versions of it. And while the sacrament of the last rites can be a big help in making the transition of death, it is not in any way necessary for admission to heaven.

For centuries, critics of Christianity have claimed that it tends to be more "churchianity" than "Christianity," and they may be right. But this is nothing new. In the time of Jesus, the corruption and arrogance of the Jewish priests led Him to expose and reprimand them. He repeatedly challenged the priests, accusing them of making a mockery of worship and spiritual living. He accused them of nitpicking about the observance of hundreds of little rules, while missing the primary purpose of religion: to know and serve God.

This led Jesus to make one of the most significant revelations of His ministry—that it is *divine love* which fulfills the law of the prophets, not obsessive obeisance to the rules and regulations of the clergy. In making this statement, He was declaring a central truth of how we are meant to relate to our Creator and worship the divine presence. The ability to express love for God and everything that God has created—especially other people—is to be the central pillar of all spiritual practices. We best serve and love God, He said, by helping others and loving one another—not by observing dead traditions, pointless rules, and empty rituals.

This was a revolutionary idea, because it was a direct hit on the bulwarks of religious bureaucracies. Jesus declared we did not need priests to live a spiritual life; what we truly need is a deep and steady love for God and His creation. If priests can help us nurture this love and refine it, then they can play a valuable role; but if they get in the way of God, as they often have, they ought to be ignored.

In fact, this is still a revolutionary idea. The Pharisees of old live on today, figuratively, in the minds and hearts of all priests (regardless of religion) who still act as if they had an exclusive franchise on God's blessings. Righteousness, isolation, and exclusivity are still commonplace in religion. We still suffer the spectacle of supposedly pious people dividing the world into the few who are saved and the vast hordes who are damned forever. These people have no idea how little they know about spirit or God's love. The American poet Edwin Markham stated the situation succinctly:

He drew a circle that shut me out.
Heretic, rebel, a thing to flout.
But love and I had the wit to win;
We drew a circle that took him in.

It is not possible to limit God's love. The narrow-minded bigots of the world will try, to be sure; they will impose rules and restrictions that keep everyone who disagrees with them out of their petty circles. But love inscribes larger circles that include even those who try to exclude everyone else.

The problem is not with rules and regulations; it is the narrow, righteous application of rules. If we apply rules in the spirit of the wisdom and love they represent, there will rarely be any problems. But if we obey only the letter of the law, we will soon be so caught up in conflict and confusion that the light of God will be lost in a bureaucratic nightmare of pettiness, arrogance, and turf battles.

Of course, it is not enough just to believe in the power of love. The Bible clearly states that "God is love." But this does not necessarily mean that we are any closer to the true expression of love than before we read those words. Indeed, few people have a full understanding of the nature of divine love. All too often, they confuse it for the human attributes of love—simple good feelings, a sense of ineffable bliss, or even fantasies about oneness with God. It is therefore important to read what the Bible says about love carefully and try to apply it to our life—not just project our own assumptions and beliefs about love onto what the Bible says.

A major explanation of the nature of love is the famous passage by Paul in chapter 13 of his first letter to the Corinthians:

> Love is patient and kind; it is not jealous or conceited or proud; love is not ill-mannered or selfish or irritable; love does not keep a record of wrongs; love is not happy with evil, but is happy with the truth. Love never gives up; and its faith, hope, and patience never fail.

> Love is eternal. There are inspired messages, but they are temporary; there are gifts of speaking in strange tongues, but they will cease; there is knowledge, but it will pass....Meanwhile, these three remain: faith, hope, and love; and the greatest of these is love.

Love does not busy itself with nitpicking, fault-finding, sin counting, or vengeance. It busies itself instead with promoting whatever is good. Nor does love tire of us and abandon us, just because we fail to recognize it; instead, it is an inexhaustible source of support and care. It comes from immortal, divine sources—not the feeble sources of our human passions.

Paul makes it very clear that the ability to experience and express the quality of love is the heart of the spiritual life. It is more important than the observation of rules, more important than inspired preaching, even more important than performing miracles:

> I may be able to speak the languages of men and even angels, but if I have no love, my speech is no more than

a noisy gong or a clanging bell....I may have all knowledge and understand all secrets; I may have all the faith
needed to move mountains—but if I have no love, I am
nothing. I may give away everything I have, and even give
up my body to be burned—but if I have no love, this does
me no good.

These are not passages to read and then forget; they contain
important revelations about the role of love in the spiritual life.
But love is not just an emotion, something we feel. It is a divine
force. As such, it is a quality we are meant to master and express
in our own life. It is not love alone, the Bible tells us, but *love in
action* that transforms us from a spiritual aspirant to a spiritual
person.

To make sure we got the point, Jesus told the story of the
Good Samaritan. A Jew is beaten, robbed, and left by the side of
the road, stripped and unconscious. A priest and a Levite, one
at a time, come upon the injured traveler, but walk on without
assisting him. A Samaritan, however, does stop to offer help. He
bandages the man's wounds and takes him to an inn, where he
pays the innkeeper to take care of the man until he has recov-
ered. To people listening to Jesus tell this story, the idea that a
Samaritan—who they would have viewed as a crude, uncivilized
person, incapable of decent behavior—would be the one to stop
would be as unlikely as a Catholic helping a Protestant in
Northern Ireland today.

In this way, Jesus hammered home the necessity to demonstrate love in acts of charity and kindness, not pious words and
sentimental gestures. Love is a force that can lift us above our
cultural prejudices and assumptions and let us deal with the real
person within every individual. It can help us mobilize the best
within ourself and put it to work when conditions demand it. But
those who put religious self-importance above the summons to
help one another are clanging bells, without love.

At a more subtle level, Jesus is also suggesting that God
comes to life on earth through kind and loving acts such as those
of the Samaritan. He "chose" the Samaritan, not the priest or the
Levite, because the Samaritan, as low as he was in the eyes of
Jews, knew what it meant to treat another person as himself. The

Samaritan, of course, chose himself; by acting charitably, he put himself on the wavelength of God. This story therefore tells us quite plainly that God's love is something far greater and more important than religious duties—or even religion itself. Religion is made for the people, not people for religion!

In spite of the obvious importance of love in the Bible, certain people never seem to tire of insisting that God does not love sinners. Indeed, to hear them talk, it would seem that God is anxiously awaiting the opportunity to condemn large portions of His own creation to hell. These people often contradict themselves without even realizing it. They mindlessly parrot the words "God loves you," only to add a very sinister "but" that instantly limits God's love and somehow excludes everyone who disagrees with them.

There is no question all of us do erect barriers between ourself and God's love. But these barriers are nothing but our own stupidity, arrogance, pettiness, malice, fear, doubt, greed, impatience, smallmindedness, and irresponsibility. God does not withdraw His love from any of us just because we are behaving like humans! The moment we overcome these flaws in our human nature, and replace them with appropriate spiritual qualities, God's love flows back into our life. It was never actually missing, of course—just obscured by our own inattentiveness.

Our relationship with God is something we control. No one can alienate us from God except ourself. No one can repair the damage and bridge the gulf of our separation except us. Divine love is a part of our spiritual nature. It is always there, a divine resource waiting to be tapped, if only we develop the ability to respond to it. As Paul wrote in chapter 8 of Romans:

> Who then can separate us from the Love of Christ? Can trouble do it, or hardship or persecution or hunger or poverty or danger or death?...I am certain that nothing can separate us from his love: neither death nor life, neither angels nor other heavenly rulers or powers, neither the present nor the future, neither the world above nor the world below—there is nothing in all creation that will ever be able to separate us from the love of God.

This is powerful statement—a statement of great hope and promise. It tells us that the most precious gift of all—God's love for each of us—is something we already possess and cannot lose. But if this is true, then why do so many people act as if it were not? Is God's love fickle? Or do we just fail to comprehend It in Its fullness?

Jesus answered these questions in His parable of the prodigal son. The younger son of a wealthy landowner demands his inheritance and immediately leaves home to travel throughout the world. He wants to enjoy life and taste of everything it has to offer. But he has no sense of the purpose of his wealth, and so he spends it foolishly on hedonistic living. Soon, the money is gone, and he is reduced to desperate poverty. He has to eke out a living as a common laborer, and ends up eating garbage left over from feeding pigs. At this point, the prodigal son realizes he has made some serious errors in judgment. He decides to return to his father's home and ask for work as a servant in the stables. He knows he has squandered his birthright and feels he has no right to be recognized as a son. So, with great contrition, he begins the long trip home.

This is a situation all of us can identify with, at least symbolically. What we may not be able to understand is the way the father reacts to the profligacy of his son. He greets his son openly and compassionately, celebrating his return with a feast and restoring him to his position as a son, not a servant. Not once does he curse him for being stupid or rebelling against his authority. He does not even threaten him with dire consequences if he ever behaves so foolishly again. Having allowed his son to make his own choices and suffer the consequences of his mistakes, the father recognizes and rejoices in the new maturity within his son.

This story of the prodigal son tells us in very clear terms that God is benevolent, generous, and eager to help us. His love never leaves us. We can stray far from the mark and end up eating scraps that not even pigs would eat. We can feel abandoned, set upon, and cheated. We may believe that God is punishing us, but in fact these are punishments we inflict upon ourself. God never abandons us. His love and guidance are with us always. And whenever we recognize our mistakes and reform our thinking and behavior, we "return" to the Father and are able to receive His blessings again.

The more we read about love in the Bible and tap it as a practical source for charitable living, the more we come to appreciate that through our love of God we establish our relationship with God. It is through love that we are bound together as one body—one body composed of billions of individual parts.

Spiritually, the race of humanity is considered to be one body—the one child of God. Some people seem to have a hard time understanding this concept, probably because they try to think of it in physical terms. But God is not a physical being. He is a universal force of love, wisdom, and strength.

Simplistic anthropomorphic images of God as a bearded old man sitting on a throne are meant to be symbolic, not literal. Obviously, one physical person cannot be the parent of the entire earth population. But God as a universal life force and source of divine love can! As Paul put it in chapter 17 of Acts:

> God, who made the world and everything in it, is Lord of heaven and earth and does not live in man-made temples. Nor does he need anything that we can supply by working for him, since it is he himself who gives life and breath and everything else to everyone....Yet God is actually not far from any one of us; as someone has said:
> "In him we live and move and exist."
> It is as some of your poets have said:
> "We too are his children."

Divine life and love are *inclusive*, not exclusive. In simple terms, this means that each of us as an individual is part of a greater life, God. We cannot be expelled from this greater life, nor can we withdraw from it. It is always with us. Just as each of our fingers is an integral part of our whole body, so also our personality and body are part of a larger organism, the greater life of God. Just as every feeling of happiness or sadness is part of the greater life of our emotions, and every memory we have is part of the greater life of our thoughts, so also the very essence of our being is part of the greater life, wisdom, and love of God.

Symbolically, we are all children of God. As Alexander Pope put it in his *Essay on Man:*

> Look round our World; behold the chain of Love
> Combining all below and all above....
> Nothing is foreign: Parts relate to whole;
> One all-extending, all-preserving Soul
> Connects each being, greatest with the least;
> Made Beast in aid of Man, and Man of Beast;
> All served, all serving: nothing stands alone;
> The chain holds on, and where it ends, unknown.

Nothing stands alone! We can never have an existence separate from God. Contrary to popular theology, there is no innate struggle between physical matter and God, or between the personality and spirit. The world is not a battleground between opposing forces known as God and the Devil. There is just God and God's light, life, and love permeating all creation and all created things. The manifestation of divine life may be incomplete and imperfect, but it *is* a constant part of our life, and we are always a part of it.

We may ignorantly *believe* that we are separated from God by an enormous cleavage, but opinion does not alter fact. Whenever we sense a cleavage of this kind, we must realize that it is a self-created illusion. We have fallen into the bad habit of paying too much attention to our physical senses and what they tell us about life. As a result, we are temporarily blind to the presence of God in our life. We need to turn our eyes and heart and mind inward once again and refresh ourself in the love and light of God.

Jesus, Paul, the prophets, and even many of our great poets have told us again and again that life on the physical plane is but a small part of God's creation. The essence of God's love and wisdom is invisible and intangible. The essence of our livingness— our capacity to be creative, compassionate, cheerful, skillful, and strong—is likewise invisible and intangible. This is the link that combines "all below and all above."

Jesus frequently made the statement that God is invisible, but that whoever had seen the Christ—God's love in action—had seen God. He repeatedly declared that He and the Father were one. In saying this, He revealed the full potential of humanity's relationship with divinity: the universal is embodied in the individual, the abstract in the finite, and God in human form.

The same relationship exists between each of us and God, although not yet fully perfected. The vast majority of us have not yet brought our human nature into complete harmony with our divine nature, as Jesus had. Nevertheless, our divine essence *is* already in complete harmony with God. It is just our character and lifestyle that have not yet been transformed into perfected vehicles for God's wisdom, love, and will. In some people, the gap between the actual and the ideal is very great. But this does not diminish the fact that all of us live and move and have our being within the greater life of God.

Divine love is not something reserved for angels and saints. It is a vital part of our being, the chain that links us all together in divine life. As such, it is meant to be an active part of our life. Unfortunately, all too many people still behave like the prodigal son, directed by wishes, selfishness, hedonism, misconceptions, and fears, instead of divine love. They have learned many lessons about what not to do, but are still wandering in the "far country" of partial ignorance and confusion. And yet, even these people have sensed the summons to return to the Father. It might come as a moment of revelation—or just as a prompting of conscience. But they have sensed that there is a light that can direct them, and whenever they catch a glimpse of it, they do try to follow it. They may be clumsy and slow, missing many opportunities to progress, but they do respond. They, too, live and move and have their existence within the greater life of God, even though they seldom realize it.

No human being is ever totally in the dark, precisely because the light and love of God is alive within each one of us, at some level. As we learn to recognize and express this treasure of love, we liberate ourself from the darkness. Instead of learning what not to do, we begin to learn what we are designed to do.

Love God—and all of God's creation.

A SERVANT OF GOD

Many devoutly religious people militantly believe that we are saved by faith alone. They claim that as long as we believe in God, we are fulfilling the major requirements of a spiritual life. Then they quote some phrase from the Bible *out of context* as evidence of the correctness of their belief. But let's look at what the Bible actually says about this type of belief, in the second chapter of James:

> My brothers, what good is it for someone to say that he has faith if his actions do not prove it? Can that faith save him? Suppose there are brothers and sisters who need clothes and don't have enough to eat. What good is there in your saying to them, 'God bless you! Keep warm and eat well!'—if you don't give them the necessities of life? So it is with faith: if it is alone and includes no actions, then it is dead.

James does not mince words: *faith without action is dead.* We have an obligation, in other words, to demonstrate our faith—as well as our goodwill, joy, wisdom, strength, and peace. A vague belief in the benevolence of God and a feeling that we are loved by God is not enough to fulfill our spiritual obligations. We must translate what we know about God into helpful, creative, and beneficent acts. We must tap the spiritual resource of **divine strength.**

Christ made the need for enlightened action clear in John 14:14: "If you love me, you will obey my commandments." These commandments are, of course, the Old Testament injunction to love God with our whole being, plus the new one He added, to love our neighbor as ourself. Jesus also gave us a number of secondary commandments—to love our enemies, to share our light and substance, and to go the extra mile without complaining—but these are essentially elaborations on the two basic commandments.

We must understand that Jesus did not just say "believe in

God." He summoned us to love God and express this love through our own love, through our own intelligence and understanding, at the level of the soul, and with every ounce of energy and skill we can muster. But we dare not reserve this love just for God; we must learn to express it as we interact with all people, even our enemies.

At the same time, we must also appreciate that an improper or ineffective demonstration of the life of spirit may actually be worse than nothing at all. The principle of demonstrating our love and goodwill is not new to the spiritual traditions of the West. Many fine people throughout the ages have heeded this message of the Christ and found creative, wonderful ways to implement it. But many others are still puzzled by what a demonstration of the inner life constitutes. As is true with many hallowed religious concepts, "witnessing for Christ" or practicing the presence of God are good ideas that are often distorted into something unspiritual. It is therefore important to have a clear understanding of what an inspired demonstration of faith, goodwill, and wisdom would be.

Perhaps the most common distortion of faith in action is that of puritanical self-denial combined with grim, guilt-driven service to the most conspicuously miserable people on the planet. Such people throw themselves into their "missions" with great zeal and fervor, but they fail in one critical way. It is not the life of spirit they are expressing, but their own grimness, guilt, and—quite often—pessimism. They are forgetting that noble deeds performed with ignoble motives—guilt, grimness, or violence—become ignoble deeds. It is not the service rendered that counts, but rather the amount of spirit that is brought to earth in the process. The Christ commanded us to act with love. If we act with grimness, guilt, self-abasement, or fear, then we cannot possibly be acting with love. Our motives betray us.

People dominated by fear, guilt, or anger tend to base any major decision they make on these feelings. What they do will therefore be strongly influenced by what they feel. The result will be a demonstration of self-absorption and defensiveness—not spirit.

There is also the problem of deliberately choosing to help those who suffer most conspicuously. There is no question that the poor, hungry, and sick need our compassionate help and generosity. But some of the people who are all too eager to help the downtrodden would laugh at the idea of helping others who suffer less conspicuously. To them, helping a genius cope with the hardships of a creative life could never be service—if the genius is so smart, let him or her figure out how to behave. In much the same way, the idea that some business people might actually perform important service through the contributions they make to society would be rejected as preposterous. As "everyone" knows, all business people are motivated by greed, not service.

This type of blindness severely limits many people in their efforts to express the life of spirit. Christ did not say, "Love only the poor." He told us to love everyone. This includes geniuses and creative people as well as slow learners. It includes the rich as well as the poor. It includes the well-fed as well as the mal-nourished. If our love and help are to mean anything spiritually, we must take off the blinders by which we have limited our efforts to act.

There are many stories in the Bible that indicate the kind of activities we should undertake as a follower of the spiritual life. Some of these activities prepare us to become more responsive to spirit. Others help elevate our awareness and understanding of life, so we can act from a more spiritual perspective. Still others indicate that we can best serve God by sharing our abundance of time, talent, knowledge, and substance with others.

The best model for spiritual activity in the Bible is, of course, the life of Jesus. It is unfortunate that untold generations of theologians have presented Jesus as an ideal we can never hope to attain. This is nonsense. The life of Jesus is carefully set forth in order to show us the ideal way to tread the spiritual path. We should therefore do our utmost to understand the meaning of His life, and try to translate this meaning into a guide for our own behavior.

The first lesson to learn from His life is that we need to prepare ourself to respond fully to spirit. Some people naïvely assume that Jesus went from being a carpenter to a great teacher overnight, but this belief is not based on the Biblical record. The

Bible makes it clear that Jesus had studied the scripture so thoroughly that he could discuss it as an equal with the most learned scholars, *even as a boy of twelve!* The fact that He was called "rabbi" by His followers and was allowed to preach in the temples also confirms a high level of training. Even the forty days He spent in the desert should be seen as part of His preparation to serve, for there He underwent tests to prove He was able to resist even the most subtle temptations of physical wealth, power, vanity, fame, and egotism.

Jesus confirmed this need for preparation in His parable of the sower of the seeds. In this story, the sower tosses his seeds indiscriminately. Some fall on the path, where birds devour them. Others fall on rocky ground where they cannot take root. Still others fall among thorn bushes, which choke out the new seedlings as they grow. But some fall on good ground, where they grow and bear much grain. This is a warning to us. If we are ignorant of the ways of spirit, we are like the hard-packed soil of a well-worn path. The seeds of spirit cannot germinate. If we are superficial, we will be like the thin soil on rocky ground, unable to sustain interest or faith in our spiritual potential once hard times arise. If we are filled with anger or worry, we will be like the thorn bushes, choking out any effort we make to grow spiritually. But if we have taken the time to prepare ourself to be receptive to spirit, by cleansing our emotions, attuning our mind, and integrating what we know about God into our values, priorities, and character, then we will be like the good soil. The seeds of spirit will flourish and will bear much fruit—we will lead a meaningful, fulfilling, and productive life.

Many of the healings the Christ performed are likewise "object lessons" instructing us in how to live. Time after time, the Christ healed by casting out demons. Even though we do not view demons in the way they were viewed two thousand years ago, there is a lesson in these healings for us. Our "demons" tend to be the dark side of our nature—the worries, obsessions, guilty feelings, jealousies, fears, grief, and self-pity that prey upon us and rob us of our vitality. It is our duty to cleanse our character of these "little rodents," as the Christ referred to them—the "thieves" that come to rob us in the night. These demons, rodents, and thieves are the forces of fear, jealousy, greed, hatred, and self-pity that can so easily undermine our well-being. Part of the responsibility of living a spiritual life is the work of eliminating these traits from our character.

The need for rising to a higher, more spiritual perspective is demonstrated in the account of the Christ calming the storm. One day, while His disciples were out in a boat fishing, Jesus was asleep in the stern. A sudden storm came up, threatening to capsize the boat. Even though the disciples were experienced boatmen, they became frightened by the intensity of the squall and woke Jesus from His sleep, imploring Him to act to save them from certain disaster. Jesus stood up and commanded the wind to be quiet and the water to be still. The squall instantly subsided, and all was calm.

This story is more than just another miracle. It is a parable telling us that we must learn to rouse our own spiritual powers and qualities from the depths of our being when confronted with the storms and stresses of life. We should not expect to be able to rely on our own skills and talents alone—we must learn to call on spirit to help us. In this regard, the turbulent winds represent the forceful currents of thought which disturb our peace of mind. The choppy waters are the anxieties and frustrations which disturb our tranquillity and threaten to capsize the ship of our life. This story makes it clear that the true source of self-mastery and self-control is the power, intelligence, and talent of the life of spirit. But this power can only be tapped if we first learn how to activate it.

One of the most moving accounts of lifting our awareness is the story of Christ raising Lazarus from the dead. There are several key elements in this story. The first is that the relatives of Lazarus were very annoyed that Jesus did not respond to their urgent requests for a healing; He had been so busy with other things that Lazarus had died. We must realize, however, that God acts on His own schedule—not at our convenience or demand. A second important clue to meaning is that when Jesus did arrive at Lazarus's tomb, He told the people to stop their wailing, then commanded that the stone covering the opening of the tomb be rolled away. These acts remind us of the need to attune ourself to the power of God by quieting our anxieties and shifting our attention away from our loss or misery and focusing it on the spiritual opportunity at hand. We must also "roll away the stone" of the doubt and disbelief entombed in our heart.

And how did the Christ raise Lazarus? He gave thanks to God the Father for hearing His request, then summoned Lazarus to come forth in the name—through the power—of God. And Lazarus did come forth, walking out with his funereal wrappings still about him.

This story represents *the principle of resurrection*, not just the fact of one man being raised from the dead. It tells us that we, too, can rise above whatever troubles us. We can learn to call on spirit to help us rise above pettiness, failures, anxieties, apathy, resentments, or anything else which seems to block our progress on the path. Even more importantly, we can learn to resurrect our dead hopes, joy, and affection, so we can once more walk among the emotionally and mentally living.

The skill of resurrection cannot be acquired, however, just by having faith that God will deliver whatever it is that we want. Over and over again, the Bible instructs us to work intelligently and lovingly to understand our spiritual nature, to purify our emotions, to illumine our mind, and to control the immature elements of our human nature. These are the tools we need to master the spiritual skill of resurrection—of lifting our awareness to a higher level.

The third lesson in demonstrating the life of spirit is learning to serve spirit in all that we do—to practice the presence of God. Few would argue against the value of this lesson, yet many people seem confused about how to learn it. They end up putting a great deal of emphasis on superficial shows of friendliness and devotion, rather than meaningful activity. They hug and kiss one another as an expression of love; they affect blissful smiles during times of devotion; and they support their friends and associates with pious platitudes. Unfortunately, this is the appearance of piety more than the practice of the presence of God. The Bible makes it clear that serving God involves making ourself useful through the daily expression of whatever skill, love, knowledge, or strength we have. It is sweet to be nice and polite, but sweetness is not necessarily a quality of spirit. It is often just a superficial gesture, motivated by the need for favorable attention from others.

This point is made abundantly clear in the parable Jesus told about the three servants. A wealthy man put three servants in charge of his property before going away on a trip. To one, he gave five thousand silver coins. To the second, he gave two thousand. The third servant received one thousand. The first two invested the money and doubled the amount while their master was away. But the third servant was afraid of losing the money, so he buried the coins to hide them. When the master returned, he praised and rewarded the two servants who had increased their money, but he cursed the one who had buried his coins, taking the money from him and dismissing him from his service.

This story emphasizes that we are given certain abilities and skills (the coins) to be used and invested so they will increase. In other words, as we use our wisdom, love, or strength in active, productive ways, our wisdom, love, and strength will increase. Our responsibilities and opportunities will expand. But if we fail to use these talents, they will shrink. We are never called on to express any quality or skill we do not have, but we are expected to take inventory of the wisdom, love, and strength we already possess and find meaningful ways to put them to work in daily life, for the good of all. It is not enough just to love God; we must demonstrate the depth of this love by taking steps to "be fruitful and multiply."

We must never underestimate the power of God's presence and blessings. We may not have the knowledge to perform miracles like Jesus did—but God does. It may be a simple miracle, such as doubling our happiness or responsibilities by the way we treat others or approach our work. Or it could be a more profound miracle. One of the most stunning miracles performed by Jesus was the feeding of the five thousand—and later on, the four thousand—with the few loaves of bread and baskets of fish His disciples had brought with them. If we tried to duplicate this miracle literally, we would be sadly disappointed. But we all have the opportunity to duplicate its inner meaning, which is to multiply our inner abundance of talent, knowledge, goodwill, and strength. Just what our strengths and talents are vary from person to person. But whatever they are, they are connected by the "chain of love" to vast sources of inner abundance. As we practice the presence of God by seeking to express these spiritual qualities and skills, we stir up the spiritual wellsprings of this wisdom, love, and power, making it possible to add these inner riches to the outer work we are doing.

If we are a teacher, we may teach only a few hundred students during our career. But if we teach with the wisdom and love of God, the impact we make on these few hundred will be spread to many, many more, as they in turn deal with others, raise children, and live their lives. This can be just as much a miracle as Jesus feeding the five thousand with the food meant only for His disciples.

The spiritual power to transform our actions in this way is always present, but it is up to us to set it in motion by taking the first few steps by ourself. Prayer and faith alone are not enough. It is the help, support, or work we perform, rightly motivated, that invokes the response of spirit. It is as if our loving service opens a door between heaven and earth for divine blessings to flow through the efforts we have begun.

The true servant of God sees the work to be done as a challenge to both the personality and spirit, working together. It takes time to achieve a level of integration where this is possible, but each of us has the potential to do so. We are designed to act in this way, combining our personal skill and talents with the abundance of spirit.

It is a combination that can produce miracles.

THE STORY OF OUR LIFE

In reading the Bible, then, we must view it as an important tool through which we can tap the intelligence, love, and strength of divine life. Like any tool, it can be used constructively and productively, or it can be misused, with harmful results. The danger of misusing the Bible lies almost entirely in taking it too seriously—in idolizing the scripture itself instead of revering the essence of divine wisdom, love, and strength it reveals. We must always take care to put nothing above God—not even the literal words of the Bible.

As we work with the Bible, we will encounter profound truths and brilliant revelations. But we need to keep two things in mind. First, we must interpret every passage of the Bible within the whole context in which it exists, not just as an individual phrase or story. The Bible is not a collection of aphorisms to be taken out of context. It is the story of spiritual aspiration. As such, we must read the whole message, not just those parts we choose to hear. Otherwise, we can be virtually certain that the brilliant revelations we receive will mislead and confuse us.

The second point to remember is that every story and teaching in the Bible has an inner dimension or significance. This inner message cannot be perceived through a literal reading of the text. It can be tapped only by reading with our *inner, spiritual eyes and ears*–our intuitive capacity to look and hear beyond simple traditions and standard beliefs and embrace the divine essence and principle being portrayed in the story or event. It was to this inner capacity to know that Jesus frequently exhorted His followers to aspire, when He said, "He who has the eyes to see, let him see" or "He who has the ears to hear, let him hear."

If we approach the Bible in this way, then it becomes much more than the inspired writings of the prophets and their disciples–*it becomes the story of our own life.* The Bible does tell us much of the history and customs of the early Jewish people, details of the ministry of Jesus, and the trials and struggles of the Apostles. But the real story of the Bible is about *us*–not any one of us personally, of course, but Everyman and Everywoman and the struggle to tap the greatness of our divine potential. Over and over, the Bible reminds us of how some aspect of human nature is usually out of harmony with divine will and love. It tells us of the virtually endless struggle within ourself, as we seek to practice the presence of God, and the often greater conflict we may encounter when we are forced to choose between our social and religious traditions on the one hand and divine guidance on the other.

Even the lives of the prophets are meant to be seen as the story of our own life–the story of our rebellion against divine will, our temptation to seek revenge, and our struggle to persevere in the face of criticism and active opposition. If we recognize ourself in these stories, then we can comprehend the spiritual principles being laid out for our study. We can likewise come to understand the structure of awareness, perspective, values, and habits which constitute our divine design and heritage.

It is this revelation—of our human nature as well as our divine birthright—that makes the Bible such a vital document for us. With a measure of vision and intelligence, we can move beyond the level of literal words and images and enter into the spiritual presence which underlies these teachings and stories. We can begin to tap the wisdom and love that inspired and led Jesus, His disciples, and the prophets. The true value of the Bible lies not in the fact that it has been revered by millions of people century after century, but that it can be a doorway to the inner teachings of love, wisdom, and strength. We need these divine qualities in order to deal with our needs, our hopes and dreams, our struggles, our passions, and our suffering. The Bible provides what we require.

What makes the Bible sacred, in short, is not the printed word itself or the proclamations of priests and theologians. The Bible is sacred because it has been able to teach generation after generation about the nature of God and our divine birthright. It is sacred because it has taught generation after generation how to bring our human nature into harmony with the divine. If we work with the Bible in this context, then its stories, parables, and teachings will come alive, in our own understanding, as brilliant metaphors for our own life, personal instruction in how to cope with the problems of our life, an intimate revelation of our inner greatness, and a glimpse into our spiritual destiny. We will tend to forget that the Bible was written thousands of years ago, and think that it was written just for us and our private needs. It will truly become the story of our life.

The Bible can be all of this—if we use it correctly. Whether we use it wisely or foolishly is entirely up to us. If we let tradition and dogma overrule our common sense, the Bible can trap us in spiritual nonsense. But if we take steps to resurrect the real meaning and significance of the Bible, then we will find that it is not just a book about divine intelligence, love, and strength.

It is a book of miracles.

Working
With Angels

The angelic kingdom is a vast realm, stretching all the way from the archangels of the Bible to the fairies and elves that tend the flowers and bushes of the fields, and help them grow. Being creatures of light and force, they are invisible to most human beings. But as we refine our senses and learn to respond more fully to divine beauty, harmony, and wisdom, we begin to register the presence, work, and joy of angelic forces. We also become aware of the possibility of working together with them.

KEEPERS OF THE GARDEN

One of our greatest cultural treasures is the vast number of arboretums, parks, and estate gardens that dot the American landscape, delighting hundreds of thousands of tourists and local lovers of flora and fauna. From spring to fall, these formal gardens are in constant bloom. The shrubs and lawns are kept immaculately manicured and clean. They are a testament to the cooperative achievements of human skill and natural beauty, working in harmony.

To a weekend visitor, such a garden might seem like a magical spot—not just because of its enchanting atmosphere and beauty, but also because flowers and shrubs seem to appear on their own, without the help of human hands or skill. This is not the case, of course. During the hours when the gardens are closed, the staff works hard to prune the shrubs, mow the lawns, transplant mature flowers that have been grown from seed elsewhere, and maintain the physical equipment. Even though we seldom or ever see these people, it is easy enough to be aware of their presence. The handiwork they have shared with us is visible testimony to their vision, skills, and labors.

In many ways, life on earth is similar to these gardens. Many aspects of our daily life are obvious and clear to us. These are the events, people, and pressures of daily living. But these aspects of life often have dimensions which are just as much hidden from view as the work force at a botanical garden. Because we do not see or hear them, we are often unaware of their presence. But they are there, interacting with us anyway. Our lack of awareness does not in any way stop them from playing their role in the great drama of the divine plan.

One of the most significant of these unseen work forces is the angelic kingdom—a group of divine workers we have all heard about but probably never seen or consciously known.

Angels are like the gardeners of the Eden we call earth; their primary work is to sustain life in the mineral, vegetable, animal, and human kingdoms of earth, even while working subtly to shape these forms and life waves so that they express more and more of the light of the divine vision. But because they work at subtle, invisible levels—even on work days—we remain virtually unaware of them. Even our clerics and theologians, who have claimed angels as their own, know almost nothing about these marvelous beings. So they debate instead their importance in scripture, betraying their total lack of direct awareness.

No matter how little we may know about angels, however, one fact remains clear. They are not only quite real, but are in fact responsible for sustaining life on this planet.

Angels are responsible for building all of the natural forms on earth, from each blade of grass to a whole mountain range—as well as the eyes we use to behold them. Angels absorb the divine forces of vitality and light and then distribute these energies to the forms in their care—be it a pine tree, a tiger cub, a chunk of quartz, or a human being. They work ceaselessly to enact and support the divine plan for the evolution of each life form and each species—as well as for the evolution of whole ecologies, nations, and cultures. Wherever something needs to grow or die, angels will be hard at work—directing, purifying, or withdrawing the life force that sustains the outer bodies.

Angels carry on this work continuously, even though we are generally unable to observe it. This blindness on our part results from the fact that we tend to think of life in terms of its physical forms—its appearance, shape, color, movement, odors, texture, and usefulness. If we cannot see it or touch it, we tend to assume that it does not exist. Angels, however, do not work directly with forms, as we do; they work with *pure force*—the subtle essences of life and vitality that animate the forms we see.

How important is this continual nurturing of the inner life of all forms on earth? Without this work performed by the angelic kingdom, there would be no life as we know it on the earth. Divine life and intelligence would be unable to manifest in form. The life of spirit would be unable to gather together the bodies it needs in order to appear on earth as a human being. The Divine Plan for creation could not be implemented.

The crucial role played by angels in planetary manifestation does not, however, lessen the value of the human experience in any way. Through our sciences, arts, commerce, and development of the mind, we are meant to discover how the secrets of earth can be unlocked and used creatively. Ideally, the work of the human kingdom and that of the angelic kingdom are meant to complement each other. Both forms of service have their origin in the intelligence of God, but angels are focused more in the gathering and distribution of the forces of life, whereas mankind is designed more to see how these forces can be translated creatively into works of culture, invention, and civilization.

The forces distributed by angels are similar to that which all of life draws from the sun—directly in the case of plants, indirectly in the case of animals. It is not just one force, but actually many subtle forces, each with a unique purpose. This is because each life form—whether it be an azalea or the Appalachians—has its own design and specific needs. The angelic kingdom is assigned the work of meeting those needs on a daily basis, keeping all of the forms of life fully charged with the energies and forces they need to survive.

Naturally, the birds and bees and grasses and shrubs of the earth are no more aware, consciously, of the tender ministrations of the angels than the average human is. Nor is there any reason why they should be. But as the average human sloughs off the cocoon of his or her absorption in form, and strives to tread the spiritual path, it does become useful to seek a direct awareness of angels. The work of spiritual aspiration, after all, requires us to become involved in the process of our own healing, growth, redemption, and enlightenment. These basic lessons must be learned first in our own mind and heart—our subtle bodies—before we can use them to help others. These are the very same bodies that the angels work with daily to refine, rejuvenate, and recharge. By learning to cooperate consciously with the angelic kingdom, even to a small degree, we can immensely increase the effectiveness of our personal growth and the spiritual service we provide.

To put this in an even more direct way, we are part of the life of the angels, and they are part of our life. The substance of our minds, our emotions, and our etheric energy system is actually borrowed from the "bodies" of angels. These angelic bodies become our bodies as they are molded and imprinted by our conscious and unconscious values, beliefs, and motives. As the angels continue to pour new vitality and energy through their bodies, we are recharged as well.

The most dramatic illustration of this interaction between humans and angels at the level of the subtle bodies is the process of birth. Angels are drawn to each new life as soon as it starts to take shape in the womb, providing the substance the new child will require. They nurture the fetus continuously, as it develops. And then, they hover over the mother at the time of delivery, establishing an atmosphere of serenity and support. For a more thorough description of the work they do in this regard, see Geoffrey Hodson's excellent book, *The Miracle of Birth.*

These same patterns are repeated during our life. Angels come to our aid when we need to heal physical or psychological injury. They assist creative people, not so much by providing ideas, but by cloaking our inspirations with the mental and astral substance that will let us translate our big ideas into successful works of art, music, and literature. Angels also stand ready to assist us at the death of the physical body, permitting our spirit and inner life to be released from the dense human body.

In all of these interactions, the angels act in harmony with the goals and plans of our soul. But since most human beings, even aspirants, are unconscious of the life of spirit, we remain unaware of the cooperation that is occurring.

Even when not interacting with humans, angels work in "response to the plan." They are guided by the force of divine destiny already established for the animal or plant in question. They do not "free lance," as individual humans would probably be tempted to do. They act according to plan.

In some cases, they act in surprising ways. The forces we call the weather are directed by huge angelic forces; massive thunderstorms are a tremendous display of angelic fireworks. Earthquakes are the by-product of movement by other angelic forces, as they seek to keep the vital forces of Mother Earth in balance. As frightening as these powerful displays can be, however, it is important to realize that they are benign. It is part of the work of tending the garden Earth.

One of the problems that has arisen in our understanding of angels is the notion that humans become angels when they die. This misunderstanding is the result of sloppy theology and sentimental Spiritualism. It is true that when humans die, it becomes more obvious that they are inhabitants of the realms of spirit. But too many people forget that a) we are inhabitants of the realms of spirit even while alive physically, and b) the realms of spirit are filled with many kinds and types of beings, all of whom would look more or less the same to the untrained, superstitious eye. To call a deceased human being an angel is something akin to calling a cat a dog, because they both live indoors.

Unfortunately, the term has been used rather loosely in translating the Bible as well. In many of the cases where an "angel" appears and delivers a message, the messenger was the spirit of a deceased human being—not a true angel. This does not diminish the meaning or value of these messages in any way; it simply clarifies an otherwise confusing event.

On the other hand, there are a variety of genuine descriptions of the appearance of angels in the Bible. When Moses performed his various acts of magic, for instance, the "pillars of fire" and "fiery wheels" were undoubtedly angels assisting in his confrontation with Pharaoh. More subtle illustrations of angelic forces at work in the Bible would be the earthquake that permitted the Apostle Paul to escape from prison—as well as the bizarre storm that caused precise, strategic damage at the time of the Crucifixion.

Actually, angels are described in virtually every major religion. In the Hindu tradition, for instance, they are known as "devas"or "shining ones," due to the effulgence of their light.

The Kabalah, the esoteric teaching of ancient Judaism, spelled out the names and duties of the major archangels. In Colossians I:15-16, the Apostle Paul clarifies their relation to the Christ or the World-Teacher: "He (the Christ) is the image of the invisible God, the first-born of all creation; for in him all things were created, in heaven and on earth, visible and invisible, whether thrones, dominions, principalities, or authorities—all things were created through him and for him."

The thrones, dominions, and principalities referred to by Paul are various orders of angels. Some of these vast intelligences are regents of invisible spheres of divine existence. Their lives are so different from ours that it strains the imagination just to speculate on it. Unfortunately, modern religion has chosen just to pretend that these Beings do not exist, leaving out all references to any levels of life standing between the omnipotence of God and life on the physical plane. This is a disservice to both human and angelic life.

It is not just the Bible that preserves a record of the angelic kingdoms, however. At the other end of the angelic spectrum from archangels and thrones are the elementals and fairy folk that make up the substance of the angelic realms in the levels of subtle form. Their lives and activities have been chronicled in fairy tales and other forms of folk lore. Although their lives are very much different than that of humans, their interests often do intersect with that of ordinary people—farmers in particular. They have therefore been viewed on occasion by humans who are gifted with some degree of clairvoyance.

Most of these elementals work closely with the elements of nature, especially plant life. They are playful in spirit, yet are shy of human contact. They bring the work of the higher levels of angelic activity down to specific plants, animals, rock formations, and so on. A more complete description of elementals can be found in Dora van Gelder's book, *The Real World of Fairies.*

From shyest sylph to the mightiest archangels, these beings of light and motion are the keepers of the garden earth. Even though invisible to our senses, they work to nurture the forms of life we use and breathe vitality into every facet of life. All life on earth depends upon the work of the angels for its sustenance.

Angels are God's assurance that the sustenance we need is being provided. Through the kingdom of the shining ones, God continues to breathe life into matter, even as He breathed life into a bit of clay and made Adam.

ENRICHING LIFE

Pessimists survey the tangible dimensions of life and presume that this is all there is. From this smallminded premise, they then leap to the startling conclusion that creation evolves without significant improvement. Some of these pessimists may grudgingly admit that there have been some achievements and breakthroughs from time to time—but nothing that has improved the quality of life. They conclude that human nature is still the same—meaning just as corrupt and spiritually bankrupt—as it was thousands of years ago. And it will be much the same thousands of years hence.

While pessimism is always chic in circles of specious thinking, it can only be sustained by looking at life—as Paul might have put it—through a keyhole darkly. Pessimists are those who have not yet learned how to climb out of the cave in Plato's famous allegory. For those who have achieved the ability to look at the broader horizons outside of the cave of human ignorance and doubt, there is no ambivalence. They can easily see that God's creation is alive and well, quietly responding to its perfect divine design. In addition, the enlightened members of humanity—as well as the entire angelic kingdom—likewise respond to this perfect design. Through them, God is constantly breathing new life into creation—new vitality, new direction, and new revelations of His plan. Creation is a living, ongoing divine masterpiece.

Most of this vitality passes through the work of the angels. If we behold life in terms that are too narrow, we may fail to grasp the nature and scope of this work. If we think of ourself only in terms of the dense physical body, for example, we will tend to discount any relevance to the need for health and vitality in our minds and emotions. To the dense materialist, after all, thoughts and emotions are just by-products of the physical life.

This perversion of the way things actually are is a cause of great confusion. Our personality consists of three "bodies"—the dense physical body with its etheric duplicate, the body of our emotions or feelings, and the body of our thoughts, the mind. The personality itself is the vehicle through which the life of spirit refines its skills and expresses its selfhood.

The substance of these three bodies is borrowed for the duration of our life from the angelic kingdom, which nonetheless is able to continue to use it for its own purposes, too. In other words, as we use the mind to think and reflect, our thoughts become cloaked in mental substance supplied to us by the angels. As we build strong feelings of devotion to God or goodwill to our friends and colleagues, our feelings are enriched with the pure substance of angelic love.

In a very real sense, therefore, the angels form a contact with divine life and light, even if we persist in denying it. Our very being and existence is intimately wrapped up in this relationship. Through these ties, and similar ones with the lesser kingdoms of life, the angelic kingdom provides the superstructure for all of life—from the notes of a great symphony to the mineral deposits in a vast desert. The spark of God ensouls matter, but it is the angelic link that enables spiritual joy to become the bloom of a flower or the smile on a baby's face.

How important is this angelic link? Without it, a diamond would never become more than a pile of carbon dust. We might be moved to express our love for a friend, but have no idea or feeling as to how to do it. This is because we humans, like all other forms of life, must work indirectly with the life of spirit. Although we aspire to the worlds of light, we are often not quite sure what they are like. We therefore depend upon the angelic link to supply us with all kinds of divine energies and ideas that we cannot reach directly on our own.

Angels, on the other hand, are constantly centered in the intelligence and love of God. It is both their design and work to radiate this intelligence and love into those life forms that must operate in the shadows, without full awareness of these inner divine resources. They are the fingers of God as He reaches out to support the sparrow in flight; they are the rhapsody of God as He sings through the heart and mind of a Beethoven or Bach.

Because angels are able to work directly with the divine plan, they are intimately involved in all facets of life on earth. In human life, for instance, they are able to breathe the life force of beauty or joy into the minds and hearts of responsive artists, musicians, poets, and sculptors. Having access to the essence of divine justice, they are likewise able to guide and inspire responsive leaders and lawmakers in our society. They can also be a great source of support for the sick, since they are attuned directly to the patterns of health for all things. Highly evolved angels can in fact embrace the spiritual destiny of a nation and breathe new life into the forces of liberty, justice, and fairness at work in the hearts of its citizens.

Indeed, the scope of the work of angels can easily stagger the human imagination, because it is so vast and powerful. Angels may oversee centuries of evolution for a whole species of animal—or the complex ecological development of life forms within a large geographic region. Some angels work at a planetary level; from our human perspective, their influence is universal. The Archangel Michael, for instance, is the angelic presence of order and justice at the mental level. He affects stability and orderly change in all forms of life, from rocks to humans and even to other angels!

From our perspective, angels are immortal. They may well work on assisting some aspect of the divine plan for dozens of centuries. Their projects may well involve many different species, generations of humans, and immense spiritual and material resources. It is hard for some people to plan accurately even ten years in advance. Angels often work on projects that will require thousands of years to complete. Our soul can understand this, because it is immortal, too. But the human personality lacks this perspective, and therefore often tries to impose its limitations on its beliefs in angels.

Even limited human beings, however, are helped by angels far beyond their expectation; they simply do not realize it. For those of us who are consciously striving to enter into the life of spirit, the benefit of learning to turn toward the help and companionship of angels can be enormous. Being in tune with divine ideas, they are in an unique position to assist us and guide us as we strive to serve the plan of God as best we can.

Some angels specialize in using esoteric sound to aid in the processes of enlightenment and healing. They inspire great composers—such as Mozart, Bach, and Mendelsohn—with magical themes that will awaken humanity to new levels of sensitivity, subtlety, refinement, harmony, and beauty. And even though it may only be the aficionados of classical music that hear some of these compositions, the impact of the angelic ministrations is registered throughout the whole of humanity, helping the entire race develop a greater sensitivity to beauty, refinement, and the life of spirit. Naturally, this impact is something that can only be studied from the inner side of life, not the outer—and it must be measured over a long span of time.

Angels likewise help artists by sharing a portion of their more refined vision or helping a responsive artist sense the inner, subtle dimensions of his or her subject. There can be little doubt, for example, that the great American artist Thomas Cole was inspired by angelic forces to recognize the living vitality of natural life—the angelic presence in nature—and infuse this dynamic perspective into his landscapes. Claude Monet is an example of an artist with a completely different style, yet in his shimmering blends of color and shape, his paintings of flowers capture as much angelic beauty and joy as the massive landscapes of Cole. His paintings convey to us a powerful message— a message penned originally by angels—that beyond the picture itself, there is a subtle but very real measure of beauty and joy within these flowers. As we behold a Monet, the beauty and joy within the painting will speak to the beauty and joy within our own inner life, and help awaken us consciously to a greater awareness of them.

The drawings of Arthur Rackham are another example of artistic angelic inspiration. Rackham became famous for his illustrations for fairy tales and other children's books. With the same impish delight often found in fairies, he captured their essence masterfully in his illustrations. Through his clairvoyant insights, we in turn are able to get a glimpse of the realities of life in the angelic kingdom. Even if we do not happen to believe in fairies or angels, the message often is able to sneak by our usual prejudices and doubts and register at subconscious levels.

The same kind of angelic influence can be found in great poetry, drama, and literature—not the kind of writing that dwells on the ills of life, but rather the kind that reveals the greater dimensions and possibilities of life. In writing about landscaping, for example, the poet Alexander Pope urged those who would build a garden to "consult the genius of the place in all"— in other words, the angelic forces which oversee and support the growth of plants, trees, and animals for this spot. He advises us to cooperate with the intelligence of nature—a clear invitation to work with angelic forces. In his classic mock epic poem, *The Rape of the Lock*, Pope is even more direct; his heroine is consciously assisted by sylphs, undines, and other fairy creatures of the angelic realm. Through the medium of humor, angelic presences are able to communicate to us openly and directly.

As in art, it is not the style of writing that reveals the angelic influence; it is the consciousness of the poet or novelist. There is a huge contrast between Pope's exquisitely refined poetry and the soaring refrains of the chants of Walt Whitman, but they each were blessed with angelic revelation. Whitman is unique in his ability to tap the angelic forces guiding the growth and development of America as a nation. He is more an American prophet than poet.

Poetry is well suited for angelic inspiration, but is not its exclusive domain. The novels of Charles Williams ring out with such clarity that it almost seems as though they were written by angels. The same is true of the nonfiction writings of Geoffrey Hodson, especially the series of books he penned describing the angelic kingdom (*The Brotherhood of Angels and Men,* et al.)

Great humanitarian organizations likewise owe much of their original inspiration and sustaining vitality to the work of angels. The ongoing work of the Red Cross is a shining example of the cooperative potential of human beings working with angels. The war relief efforts that followed both world wars also illustrate how effective guidance from angelic realms can be when it is necessary to meet the urgent needs of huge segments of humanity in times of crisis.

Similar patterns of inspiration and revelation can be found in great scientific breakthroughs. This is particularly true in the areas of animal husbandry, horticulture, electricity, and unlocking the potential of minerals. Not only are scientists discovering ways to make our vegetables and animals more fruitful and productive, they are also discovering new ways to use these natural resources to improve the quality of life. The renaissance in the use of subtle energies for medical treatments is a good example of work that is partly inspired angelically. Since one of the basic duties of angels is the direction of force, they are uniquely suited to help us unlock the secrets of manipulating the subtle forces of the body and mind, to accelerate the healing of both.

Naturally, as science becomes more global in scope, the need for intelligent cooperation with angels will become increasingly important.

This kind of global rapport is also important as we strive to serve the destiny of our nation. From the perspective of angels, human society is a divine life wave that needs to be purified, focused, and motivated. Since this kind of work is exactly what angels are designed to do, it is only natural that they are highly involved in shaping the destiny and development of nations. Depending upon the need of the moment, the angelic forces will either be deeply immersed in peacemaking efforts—or they will be busy stirring up rebellion and revolution, when nothing less will cleanse a society of a corrupt bureaucracy and rigid traditions.

For many people, it will be difficult to accept the idea that angels could work through us so readily without us even knowing about it. These are the very people most in need of a new revelation about life, of course—and the least likely to receive it. Like most unimaginative materialists, they assume that what they cannot sense simply does not exist—and what they do not understand cannot work. Yet they have no trouble learning to use a television, even though they do not understand how it works—and are unable to see television waves. They somehow manage to accommodate themselves to a widely accepted phenomenon.

In much the same way, we can assume that we do not need the ability to register the presence of angels directly in order to accept them as part of divine life and learn to work cooperatively with them. If we can attune to their intelligence, love, and light, we will be able to interact with them to a surprisingly large extent. And it is to our advantage to learn how to do just this, for even the smallest degree of cooperation with angels will enrich our livingness in many wonderful ways. Angels can help us to understand more about the life of spirit and how it is designed to function in our life. They can assist us in our creative efforts—as well as our exploration of the inner dimensions of life. And they can be especially helpful in any effort we make to bring renewed health to our loved ones—or ourself.

The challenge of working consciously with angels is enormous. Fortunately, so are the benefits.

COOPERATING WITH ANGELS

As Alexander Pope put it, "Fools rush in where angels fear to tread." Whenever we hear of something new, our human nature tends to want to be the first to have it. In our foolishness and arrogance, we sometimes rush into new experiences, new relationships, and even new ideas a bit too rapidly.

This impulsive approach will not work in learning to cooperate with angelic forces, even fairy folk. We cannot demand that they come to us; we cannot lay traps for them and capture them in bottles, like the jinns or genies of ancient fable. They will choose when to approach us, and the conditions under which we will work together.

The key is the very simple word, "cooperation." The angels will not let us boss them around—or experiment with them, as so many scientists are wont to do. They have no interest in satisfying our idle curiosity. They turn a blind ear to our greed and quest for fame and recognition. But if we have a genuine intent to work in harmony with them, on their own wavelength, then there is no limit to the relationship we can develop.

It is important to understand that the elementary practices of spiritual growth may not work in attracting the help of angels. Simple faith and surrender to spirit may help build a tie between the personality and the higher self, but it is unlikely to attract any angelic forces. Angels do not care if any of us believe in them; they exist whether we believe or not. What they are looking for in terms of human collaboration are spiritual adults who have established spiritual priorities, purified their character, and proven that they can think and act in harmony with the divine plan.

In short, the key to building a cooperative relationship with angels at any level is the ability to engage in creative work of a high caliber—to create in the mode of spirit. This does not mean that we must be an artist or dancer to work with angels. Spiritual creativity embraces the whole range of working with divine ideas and forces to build on earth that which is in heaven.

But even the right intent and right skill are not enough. We must also create the right atmosphere in which to receive the angelic visitation. If we are preoccupied with worry or anger, no angel is going to want to work with us. If we have damaged our subtle bodies through wanton exposure to hard rock or rap music, no angel will want to be close to us.

On the other hand, the effort to create or perform refined, harmonious music—or radiate loving assistance and support to others—would go a long way toward creating an ideal atmosphere in which to entertain angels of all degrees.

In short, we need to build a strong mental structure of spiritualized consciousness. We must prove ourself ready to work with angels by weaving a tapestry of human qualities that will enable us to work side by side with angels. The contents of this structure will vary somewhat with each person, but the primary qualities that must be included are: wisdom, knowledge, creative talent, enlightened motives, integrity, constant aspiration, steady goodwill, and persistent effort. As we master each of these spiritual qualities, we take another step toward full cooperation with angels. So let's examine each step a bit more fully.

Wisdom is the beginning point. If we are to work with angels and share the forces they wield, we must be capable of responding to the divine design for the work being done. Our efforts must be guided by this inner plan—not by pleasant whimsies or metaphysical speculations. Wisdom is not the product of idle theorizing or public opinion. It is the ability to interact with the divine plan at its own level and retain the clarity of this vision, unclouded by materialistic assumptions, emotional delusions, or ignorant speculations. This ability becomes possible when the individual is able to function at least to some degree as a soul in waking consciousness—that is, when he is able to comprehend the perspective and intent of the soul and harness the personality to express this spiritual intent without distortion.

Even among spiritual aspirants, this measure of wisdom is extremely rare. It is never found among less evolved people. The average human being is so stuck in satisfying his or her own needs and emotional comfort that spiritual wisdom becomes impossible. In fact, viewed from the level of spirit, ordinary people are rapidly drowning in the tidal wave of their own sentiments, aware only of what their senses are telling them and missing completely the subtle messages of the spiritual will.

Wisdom is something more than the accumulated insights of a busy life on earth. It is the accumulation of insight gained as the soul has learned more about the divine plan—its design, purpose, and perspective—and found ways to express these insights through the relationships, challenges, and opportunities to be useful of an enlightened personality. It presupposes a certain amount of mastery in self-awareness, purification of the mind and emotions, and the illumination of our understanding. These, of course, are the achievements of a lifetime dedicated to spiritual living—not just wish fulfillment or theorization.

As wisdom emerges, we gain a spiritual perspective on the vast evolutionary schemes that direct the work of angels. This measure of insight becomes the first link in true cooperation—as well as providing a profound grasp of the awesome scope of the divine plan. It is the kind of wisdom embodied by Thomas Jefferson and a few of the other Founding Fathers of America. They were consciously aware that they were setting new standards for government—a government designed to embody the will of the people while responding to the mandates of the divine plan. Many of the Founding Fathers were strong willed individuals, but enough of them had sufficient contact with the divine intent—and the wisdom to recognize it—to put aside the squabbles and lay a strong foundation for government. As a result, they were able to cooperate both with the divine plan and the angelic forces working upon it to establish a new nation.

Knowledge and creative talent. To be effective, wisdom must be combined with knowledge and creative talent—the ability to connect divine will with our personal will, divine intelligence with our human intelligence, and divine love with our individual love.

The level of knowledge required for interaction with angelic workers is the ability to work comfortably and consciously at archetypal levels, moving back and forth between abstract and concrete thoughts. We must be able to define the needs of humanity and the world in terms of the divine plan, not just popular opinion.

Our creative talents likewise must surpass the ordinary level, defined as it is by the expectations of our culture. To work with angels, we must be able to seize the solar breeze of an incoming evolutionary force, comprehend it, and then translate it into a vision we can share with others. It is not uncommon for work of this nature to require several lifetimes to accomplish, especially since the work is not apt to receive popular support, at least in the beginning stages. In fact, we may have to stand against "socially correct" ideas and fads, thereby incurring criticism or even condemnation.

A hint of this kind of creativity can be found in the works of writers such as Charles Dickens or Victor Hugo, whose stories stirred up the latent goodwill in the masses and inspired the intelligensia of the day to institute long overdue reforms. These writers shook the very pillars of church, government, and the legal system—not through their own intervention, but by rallying their readers to demand change. In this way, new spiritual light and love was invested into mass consciousness, and through it into the institutions of church, government, and education.

Many people strive to reform society in similar ways, but have not yet developed the knowledge or the creative talent required. They have good intentions and compassion for others, but neither of these qualities can achieve much all by themselves. Only when our compassion and dedication is blended with wisdom, knowledge, and creative skill can we attract the cooperative assistance of angelic forces that we need to succeed.

It is the support of angelic forces that can make one individual a mighty power, indeed.

Enlightened motives are another important element in making ourself ready to cooperate with angels. A motive is any force that impels us to act. In the average person, motives are highly selfish and personal—ambition, vanity, or fear. The spiritual aspirant begins to learn about the need for more refined motives, but mostly just cloaks his personal motives in a spiritual disguise. This is not enough, if we intend to work side by side with angels. Angels are motivated by the divine plan itself. If we hope to work with them, we must make the leap and learn to be motivated in this way as well. We must learn to work and act impersonally.

Some sentimental people misinterpret "impersonal" to mean

cold and uncaring. This, however, is a gross distortion of an important spiritual posture. A person who is motivated impersonally is one who is able to work solely for the intrinsic merit of the project, not because he or she is expecting personal glory, wealth, or power—or is trying to atone for a massive amount of fear, guilt, shame, or self-pity. He is motivated only by the desire to be helpful.

The benefit of enlightened motivation is that it frees us to deal exclusively with the work to be done. We do not have to take time off to placate our neurotic tendencies or play a hundred different roles to suit all our friends and enemies. We have the strength to do the work that needs to be done and not be distracted by unimportant side issues.

It is easy to be distracted by unimportant motives—and almost always fatal to our effectiveness as an agent of light or a co-worker with angels. The classic case is that of someone who goes to a lawyer for help in settling a dispute with another person. The lawyer almost always imposes new motivations on the situation—i.e., winning the case, humbling the other side, and forcing them to make concessions. Instead of serving justice, we are now trying to ram it down their throats. The once-neutral motive of trying to settle a dispute becomes clouded with self-serving motives.

This type of distortion is deadly to enlightened work. Angels do not have the kind of personalities capable of vanity, selfishness, or worry. They have no hidden agenda except to serve as a willing and competent servant of divine intelligence. Their fulfillment lies in completing their work, nothing else. They are indifferent to personal affection, flattery, and criticism.

An excellent example of a person who was able to operate with enlightened, impersonal motives without sacrificing his vision was Winston Churchill. For fifteen years, he was out of step with the dominant thinking of England—but he refused to bend in his convictions that Hitler must be contained and deposed. Even after he became prime minister, he was under great pressure to compromise and pander to public fears. Most men would have, just as Neville Chamberlain did. But Churchill remained detached from these pressures, convinced that there was only one right course for his country, his king, and his God.

To work cooperatively with angels, we need to strike a similar posture. Our work needs to be motivated by altruistic principles, not our desire for personal gain. We need to be able to complete our work even in the face of disappointment, criticism, and opposition.

Integrity is another indispensable quality to cultivate in anticipation of working with angels. As it applies to spiritual work, integrity is the ability to remain true to the divine ideas that inspire us, and not let them be contaminated or dissipated by popular ideas, trends, or delusions. Richard Wagner, for example, was uncompromising in how his operas were to be conducted and staged. Johannes Brahms destroyed large numbers of his compositions rather than publish anything beneath his standard of excellence. Luther Burbank, the great horticulturist, turned down large sums of money and grand promises and refused to sell out to people who wanted to capitalize on his fame and record. These creative giants all demonstrated an ability to honor and remain true to the source of their inspiration.

This kind of integrity is important because angels are not interested in working through unreliable sources. The strength and depth of one's integrity must be well proven before significant chances to work cooperatively will emerge.

Constant aspiration to the highest must likewise be demonstrated as an integral part of our character. Angels are able to participate in the distribution of divine force because they can identify with it in its highest octave. We live in a world where awareness of the highest and purest is not automatic. We must therefore learn to rise above the lower octaves of human expression and constantly be mindful of the best.

We remain mindful of the best mentally by adhering to the commandment to love God with all our mind.

We remain mindful of the best emotionally by adhering to the commandment to love God with all our heart.

In other words, as we think upon who we are, the work we do, the duties we serve, and the colleagues we assist, we strive always to define these things in terms of their noblest elements. We eschew gossip, rumor, self-pity, and defensiveness in favor of identifying with the cosmic ideal we ought to be serving.

Outstanding examples of constant aspiration to the highest

can be found in the lives of people such as Albert Schweitzer and Beethoven. Schweitzer was already a famous musician and theologian in Europe when he decided to study medicine so he could serve in Africa. He gave up a comfortable life of fame and honors in order to serve the plan as he perceived it. Beethoven continued to compose great music even after he became totally deaf. Others would have used their handicap as an excuse for self-pity and retired from public life. But Beethoven chose not to let a physical deficiency interrupt his spiritual service.

Steady goodwill creates a climate of benevolence which makes it possible to link our consciousness with angels and other spiritual workers. Indeed, goodwill is the keynote on which all spiritual work is generated. This force of goodwill, however, should not be confused for the "warm fuzzies," self-contentment, and nice feelings so commonly touted in spiritual circles today. It is the corollary to aspiration: having identified the highest and noblest within any person, project, or cause, we extend our love and dedication to helping it grow and become stronger. Goodwill is therefore the guiding principle that overshadows our efforts—the atmosphere of gentleness and kindness that helps nurture the work we do.

The power of goodwill is that it shields our spiritual endeavors from the pollution of mass consciousness and the dark side of human nature. It also helps sustain our link with the realm of spirit and the archetypal forces of the mind of God. In a very real sense, it is this aura of steady goodwill that opens the door for true contact and cooperation with the angels. It is also an indispensable attribute for anyone who seeks to heal the sick, whether individual people or society as a whole.

One of the most powerful demonstrations of the expression of goodwill is that of Abraham Lincoln, who demonstrated an unusual measure of generosity of spirit and tolerance even in the midst of terrible conflict. He was assailed by his supporters almost as much as by his critics, yet remained a calm, healing force with a vision of what the United States could become.

Persistent effort is the ability to sustain continual effort in working with angels and spirit for long periods of time. No plan, no matter how noble, and no intention, no matter how divine, means anything unless it produces some measure of transformation or growth. In other words, we must be able to initiate productive activities and guide them toward meaningful results. Heaven must be done on earth.

The need for persistent effort will be immediately clear to anyone who has accomplished any important goal. But oddly enough, there are many people on the spiritual path who do not cherish persistent effort. They believe that holding a spiritual idea or vision in their mind is all they need to do to serve the plan of God. It is not just our duty to ask for greater light and love on earth, as though we were sending in a purchase order to Headquarters. It is our duty to get busy and apply our skills in intelligent, persistent ways. It is our duty to convert enlightened thoughts and attitudes into enlightened productivity.

In fact, the physical plane is the one area in which we can make a contribution that the angels cannot. We have the hands to build with; they do not. They can perform their daily functions without our help, just as we can perform ours, if we choose, without them. But the possibilities that can be achieved if we learn to work together, cooperatively, are so great that it behooves each of us to explore this opportunity more completely.

These are the steps we must master to be able to work effectively with angels. They can be summed up in one key idea: we must *rise up* to their standards of work. We must build a structure of consciousness that enables us to share—to some degree—their cosmic perspective and sense of the universal.

Making the effort to do so opens up not only the kingdom of angels but also the higher levels of spirit as well. It helps us begin to understand the vast power within the divine plan—and the role we are summoned to play in it.

THE PRESENCE OF ANGELS

The opportunity to cooperate with angels, of course, is nothing new; they have been a part of the human experience for many millenia. But most of this interaction has occurred—and still does—without our conscious knowledge. It is the ability to cooperate consciously that is slowly changing, creating new possibilities for the spiritual aspirant. It is not changing because

God has had pity on us. It is changing only because more and more humans are developing the ability to work and act as spiritual adults. As this development progresses, so will our awareness of angelic life.

Our knowledge of angels is still clouded by many misconceptions. Some people think that angels quit visiting humans two thousand years ago; others believe that if an angel were to appear, it would be with a crack of thunder, a blinding flash of light, and a deep voice chanting, "Fear not!" As might be expected, however, angels seldom indulge in such theatrics. Their presence can be quite real in our lives, yet at the same time unfelt and unseen. They hover over pregnant mothers to supervise the building of the subtle bodies of the fetus. A different order is on hand at the time of death, making the transition easier for the dying person. These services are offered automatically; we do not need to be aware of them to receive them.

In between birth and death, there are many other ordinary kinds of experiences which might well draw unseen angels to help us quietly. A sincere effort to heal another person or an area of disease in society is one of the most common ways we attract the interest—and help—of angels. A deep love for music—as well as the talent to perform it—would readily draw the attention of the angels of harmony. The sincere effort to teach others and help them grow could likewise attract assistance from these beings of light. Even in times when we find ourself caught up in unjust circumstances, and must take a stand as an agent of justice, we may well be helped by these unseen forces—if we are doing it right.

Doing it right is an important key. If we blame society for our woe, we will repel any angels that might help. If we seek justice as a cover for vengeance, we will likewise cut off any possible support from these realms. If we are motivated only to save ourself, and not correct the larger injustice being served, the angels are apt to leave us to ourself.

It is not necessary to pray or chant to attract this help. As we rise up into our higher self and try to love the ideal we seek to serve—the harmony of our music, the growth of the child, the perfect health of our friend, or the principles of divine justice, the keynote is sounded. The proper order of angels will respond, *provided that we have created an atmosphere that welcomes them.*

This is what most self-appointed reformers fail to do. They are dedicated to change—but are not willing to submit to the divine plan. They are interested in justice—but only for themselves or the aggrieved party they have chosen. They want to help humanity—by forcing it into a mold of their own choosing.

These people will continue to perform their "public service," of course, but without the assistance of angels or other divine resources. They may even become quite famous. But their efforts will not bear long lasting fruit. Often, in fact, it fosters more division and discontent than forward progress.

This scenario changes whenever any of these people awakens to the presence of spirit within them. As they learn to respond to the soul and its plans more than the whims and proposals of mass consciousness, then interaction with the realms of angels becomes possible. Of course, their style of pursuing reform changes as well. Instead of trying to enforce change on others, they learn to inspire others to exercise more responsibility. Instead of advocating revolution, they learn to use the power of proper authority for change and transformation. They learn that the authority to initiate change is derived from the archetypal levels of creation—not the frustrations of mankind.

In other words, these people learn to approach the problems of life creatively. Instead of just recycling old traditions and chasing old goals, they are able to offer fresh ideas and new ways to solve old problems. They become a channel through which the vitality of the divine plan can flow into the earth plane.

It is when this change occurs that people begin to attract the interest of angelic forces, even though they will probably not realize it. The angels help them develop their sense of vision, so that they understand more clearly what the divine plan is trying to accomplish. They may also provide a certain measure of vitality or vigor, so that others will be attracted to the dynamism of the project or activity.

Even though much of this assistance may be rendered without our knowledge, it would be a mistake to assume that cooperation with angels is automatic. Even if we make a deliberate effort to operate on their wavelength, they may make an equal effort to ignore us. We must keep in mind that many human customs are incompatible with the ways of angels. While we may get a kick out of negotiating or presenting complex business proposals, angels may well be repulsed by such hurly-burly scheming. To angels, the thought of getting an advantage over others or haggling over differences is utter nonsense. Such attitudes would indicate that we are not yet ready to cooperate with angels.

Undoubtedly the easiest avenue for becoming aware of the presence of angels is through religious ceremony. Ritual invocation, when properly performed, is designed to draw in assistance from the appropriate order of angels, whether we are celebrating a marriage, baptism, communion, or an ordinary worship service.

This only makes sense. Humanity is apt to be at its highest level of aspiration, goodwill, and wisdom during a time of religious celebration. It is therefore easier for angels to approach. Secondly, the congregation is more likely to be united in a common thought of healing, blessing, or rejoicing, thereby allowing the angels to work in harmony with them.

This does not mean that every religious ceremony is attended by angels. The celebrant—priest, rabbi, or minister—must be competent and the liturgy must be inspired, as well as inspirational. These conditions occur less frequently than they ought to, but nonetheless the potential is always there.

Ideally, the celebrant will have the strength to lift the rest of the congregation to high enough levels of aspiration that they, too, may sense the angelic presence filling the church or synagogue. Even if the celebrant is unaware of connections with the life of spirit permitting this, his or her devotion to the divine and all that it represents may be enough to make the invocation work.

The role of the liturgy in these formal celebrations is to invoke a divine blessing from God and to evoke from us the qualities of consciousness we need to cultivate in order to honor our communion with the angels—the qualities of wisdom, knowledge, enlightened motivation, aspiration, goodwill, and persistent effort. The liturgy should ask us to acknowledge the authority of divine light and love above all else in our life. It should also give us the opportunity to rededicate ourself to expressing these qualities in all that we do.

There is a real art behind the composition of effective liturgy. If the liturgy is meant to summon angels, the very structure of our invocation needs to create a figurative "funnel" that stretches upward toward the spiritual forces we seek to contact, and downward to provide a conduit for divine force to be poured upon us. As the liturgy unfolds, step by step, it is meant to construct an actual thought-form of this nature out of the aspiration and devotion of the congregation. If the celebrant is thinking about dinner after the service, however, and the congregation is wondering who will win the ball game that afternoon, the liturgy will fall short of its purpose. As a result, the celebration may not become strong enough to invoke the angelic hosts—nor provide a channel through which divine power can be poured.

Obviously, the more the celebrant and the members of a congregation consciously dwell on the prospect of an angelic presence at their worship, the more likely it is that their efforts will be rewarded. It should also be added that the inability to summon angels does not negate other aspects of a worship service; it is not necessary to attract angels in order to honor God and be guided by the life of spirit. Nonetheless, the inclusion of angels in any worship service is a powerful way to enrich the meaning of the celebration.

In our daily life, in fact, it might be a distraction to try too hard to contact angels. It would be better just to seek out the assistance of the life of spirit in general and not be concerned with which spiritual agency might answer our prayer. In seeking support and insight at work, for example, we might ask:

May the light of God guide
And the love of God support
The work I do today.

At other times, we might want to focus on a specific quality or archetypal force, such as divine justice or healing. Then we might want to proceed by saying:

May the powers that bring healing and comfort
Be with the sick and discouraged
To bring strength and healing to mind and body
Insofar as it is possible.

Or, in the case of a need for justice, we might say the words:

Let divine justice and order
Regulate the affairs of men and nations,
Dissolving divisions and creating harmony.
Let goodwill guide all who would seek peace.

Of course, these simple prayers could be said by two different people with widely different results. If intoned by an insincere person, for the purpose of impressing others with his piety, the effectiveness of the prayer will be nil. When intoned by a person with a skillfully constructed consciousness of the divine, however, the results will be immediate and powerful.

It is not our belief in spirit and in angels that brings the result, after all. It is our level of consciousness and preparation and readiness. Have we made a dedicated effort to purify our emotions, illumine our mind, and enlighten our lifestyle? If we have, there is much we can share with all facets of spirit, especially angels. But if we have not, our beliefs will remain unfulfilled—until we rectify the omission.

THE VISION

In the centuries to come, as more and more people are able to think and act as souls, rather than personalities, there will be greater measures of cooperation between humans and angels. It is part of the evolutionary plan for humans to assist or take over the work of angels in a variety of ways. Healing, for instance, will one day be performed by carefully trained priests who will summon and direct angelic forces to repair human bodies, instead of using medicines or surgery. The regulation of the weather—and much of the problem of pollution—will become possible as enough enlightened people emerge that they can be taught how to summon the various angels who control the weather and the quality of air, water, and soil. Eventually, it will even be possible for fire departments to put out fires by performing ceremonies that compel the fire angels to retreat!

These developments, of course, belong to the far distant future. They are so remote that they serve only to whet our imaginations. Yet they do hint at the tremendous potential that awaits us when we learn to work in harmony with angels.

They teach us something of great importance, too. Where there are fires ablaze in our life—anger that is raging out of control or fear that threatens to consume us—we can call on spirit to put it out. It may not be a fire angel that responds, but the life of spirit is replete with agencies that can douse a wildfire in our own life. Just so, there are other spiritual agencies—and angels—that we can call on to control the inner storms of our moods and emotions. And prevent a few inner earthquakes as well! Let us therefore learn from the example of the angels. They do not debate theology; they know God. They do not try to coerce one another into thinking as they do; they serve God. They do not try to remake the world; they love God.

We, too, are asked to know God, to serve God, and to love God. And as we do, we will discover something quite wonderful. We share this duty with the angels.

The Work
Of The Hierarchy

The soul of humanity is the Hierarchy, which acts as a single great individual to inspire and nurture the creative works of mankind—in government, the arts, science, the healing arts, business and commerce, education, and religion. The tools this one Creative Person uses to fulfill the divine Plan symbolically represent each of these seven great institutions of society.

THE SOUL OF HUMANITY

From Plato to Ralph Waldo Emerson, the great thinkers of humanity have recognized that the full spectrum of human livingness is complex and multi-layered. They have understood that human life does not just consist of family, career, material possessions, and personal happiness. They have likewise grasped that it involves far more than the anguish, suffering, and frustration that dominate so many people. Whether or not we are conscious of it, each of us has a rich inner core of values, wisdom, compassion, joy, and strength which persists and grows regardless of what is happening in our daily lives. Some people call this rich inner core of life the soul; others refer to it as the higher self, the good within us, and in many other ways. The label we use is unimportant, of course—but the role this inner essence plays in our life is anything but. It is nothing less than the creative core of life within us—the source of our wisdom and conscience, the root of our goodwill and compassion, and the heart of our humanitarian skills and qualities. It is also our direct link with the life of spirit—and God.

Is the human soul just a construct in the fertile imaginations of people like Plato and Emerson—or is there proof that it actually exists? Being abstract, the reality of the soul cannot be proven through standard scientific tests of measurement and analysis in a laboratory. But proof does exist—objective, reproducible evidence that confirms the reality of the human soul. This proof is found in the testimony of hundreds of human explorers in the realm of spirit throughout civilization's history—great figures who have toiled in the fields of healing, personal development, and creativity and have extended the scope of human knowledge and achievement. These people, from all different cultures and all different times in human history, unite as with one voice to confirm the reality of the soul. Each in his

167.

or her own way has discovered that the true work of healing, growth, and creativity is driven by something much greater than his or her own skills and insights. It is fueled by inner wellsprings of love, joy, inspiration, and strength which transcend existing cultural traditions.

It might be argued that the testimony of these people is anecdotal—their experiences were not controlled by rigorous scientific procedures. But no scientific laboratory has ever produced a Rembrandt painting, a piece of writing as inspired as the Declaration of Independence, an exemplary life such as that of St. Francis, an act of heroism on the battlefield, or a healing such as those performed by Padre Pio. The scientific laboratory is a place for studying and analyzing physical phenomena. The human mind and heart are also legitimate laboratories—not for studying white mice and monkeys, but for exploring the inner dimensions of human life. They are laboratories of creativity— workshops of spirit. It may be true that only a small fraction of the billions of members of humanity has ever done serious work in these laboratories—but this is precisely the reason why their reports are not just anecdotes. They are evidence—the only compilation of evidence humanity has. As such, it should be seen as the richest treasure of our civilization.

But it is not just the individual human that possesses a soul. The human race as a whole—civilization—has one as well. At the level of our personalities, we tend to emphasize our differences and eccentricities. We fight with one another, engaging in petty strife. But at the level of the soul, we discover that the human nature of the billions of people on the planet—as well as the billions not physically alive at present—is somehow interwoven, linking us all in a common purpose. There is a rich, inner essence of humanity which embodies the collective genius and capacity for transcendence of the whole race. Emerson called it the Oversoul. Just as our individual indwelling soul provides the life force and plan for our evolution, work, and growth in each incarnation, this Oversoul supplies the power and plan for the growth and work of humanity as a whole—civilization.

The differences between the soul of an individual and the soul of the whole human race are both quantitative and qualitative. While our individual soul oversees and nurtures the growth and achievements of one personality, the soul of the human race oversees and nurtures the evolution and accomplishments of human culture worldwide. While our soul generates a plan and design for personal work and activity, the soul of the human race develops plans and design for the work and activity of the whole race—and its civilization.

Emerson was not the first to label this collective soul of humanity. In fact, it has been known by many different names by thinkers and writers in many cultures. But the traditional name that has been used to refer to it, from the days of the Greek temples on, is the Hierarchy of Mankind.

The Hierarchy of Mankind is not just a collection of human souls, as a hive would be a lodging place for bees. Just as the individual soul is far greater than its personality, being the inner essence of it, the Hierarchy is far greater than just the sum of all human beings—even greater than the sum of all human souls. It connects us with universal life—the life of spirit. Esoterically, it could be thought of as a vast intelligent life form which acts through the human race but is older and more evolved than humanity. It is, in fact, a distinct kingdom of life—the fifth kingdom. In the long process of evolution, there are five kingdoms we interact with as humans. Each represents a more refined expression of consciousness. The first kingdom is mineral life. The second kingdom is plant life. The third kingdom is animal life. The fourth kingdom is human life. The fifth kingdom is the Hierarchy.

The Hierarchy is not *directly* active in human affairs. Instead, it works through agents—enlightened individuals, both in and out of incarnation—who serve as guardians of the Plan for the evolution of the human race and civilization. These representatives embody or are guided by one or more of the aspects of spirit, such as love, wisdom, creativity, purpose, or harmony. As a result, they are able to lead humanity and its culture along the routes of growth and development set forth in the Plan for the orderly unfoldment of civilization.

Viewed from the top down, the head of the Hierarchy is the World Teacher. In the West, we usually label this agent as the Christ, but He is known by other titles in different cultures throughout the world. The true nature of the Christ as World

Teacher is not exactly the same as the average Christian imagines Jesus, whose work has been stereotyped as though frozen in time and space by one brief ministry. The World Teacher is universal in scope and influence; He is a living force which greatly transcends what Westerners generally regard as the historic Jesus, as great as that is. This more complete nature of the Christ is hinted at in the Bible when it refers to Jesus as "the teacher of men and angels." As such, the Christ is the director of the Hierarchy and the evolving life and work of all humanity, plus all of the works of civilization.

If we view the inner life from the perspective of an intelligent person incarnate in physical life, then the Hierarchy is the structure of wisdom, purpose, cohesive love, and the life of the human race. It is the transcendent essence from which springs the collective wellspring of inspiration and guidance for the entire race. It expresses itself primarily through the major institutions of society and the creative achievements of our culture.

Just as human civilization is not monolithic, but broken down into a variety of disciplines, the Hierarchy is likewise organized in various divisions. This departmentalization focuses the immense power and authority of the Hierarchy into areas of specialization, each with its own set of representatives. Each subgroup remains united with all of the others in their common purpose, but concentrates its efforts primarily in its area of specialization. These departments correspond more or less to the activities that we would call science, the arts, education, commerce, religion, government, and health. It is the Hierarchy that is responsible, behind the scenes, for developing long range plans for the development of these great enterprises of human activity. Agents of the Hierarchy can be found working busily to guide these developments in each of these areas of human endeavor at all times, in all lands throughout the globe.

Just as the basic nature of the Christ is inclusive love and charitable service, the keynote of the Hierarchy's essence and motivation is likewise goodwill. In other words, even when the interest of the Hierarchy is focused in an area such as commerce or science, the clear sign of Its involvement would be activities that are based on an inclusive love for the highest potential for goodness in all aspects of human culture and civilization.

Movements that enslave the minds and hearts of men and women—or emphasize materialism at the expense of spirit—would not be programs supported by the Hierarchy, no matter how much such groups might cloak themselves in the appearances of compassion or helpfulness.

It is even more important to realize that the Hierarchy is not some ineffable blob of bliss that sends us unconditional love. Its true nature is very much different. It is a vast network of intelligence, power, and goodwill that serves as the creative nexus and the headquarters for the evolution of our race and the development of civilization. It is the actual, although hidden, government of the world, nurturing the development of human character and overseeing the innovations of science, government, the arts, education, religion, commerce, and health. It embodies and implements the Plan for the spiritual destiny of the human race.

It is impossible to overestimate the importance of the Hierarchy. For us humans, it is both heaven—our divine origin and destiny—as well as the bridge which links the earth with heaven. It is what we are becoming.

BEHIND THE SCENES

The primary work of the Hierarchy is to infuse all human institutions with spirit. It therefore works to promote goodwill, enlightened understanding, and mature behavior wherever It can. Due to the scope of Its operations, however, the Hierarchy tends to work through *groups,* rather than individuals. Even when popular opinion tends to lionize the work of a single individual, such as Albert Einstein in physics or Mother Teresa in religion, the individual agent is not just free lancing on his or her own. Such agents are working as part of a larger group or department of the Hierarchy, even though they may not be consciously aware of the larger network supporting their efforts.

Sometimes agents of the Hierarchy come together on the physical plane and work cooperatively with one another, as was the case with the Founding Fathers of America. At other times, the agents are widely scattered and have little or no direct contact with each other, as was the case with the many scientists who made key contributions to the development of the radio in the late nineteenth century. They were all being inspired by the same source—the Hierarchy—even though they were working in various remote parts of the world. Their association with each other as a group existed only at an esoteric, inner level.

All departments of human civilization are linked to the Hierarchy in this manner. This idea may come as a surprise to some, who believe that religion is the primary agent used by the Hierarchy for revealing or infusing spirit into our society. In reality, *all* of the major institutions of society can be effective and powerful vehicles for distributing the wisdom, love, and will of the divine Plan into human character and civilization. Working with the life of spirit involves much more than the pious rituals and dogmatic proclamations of religious sects. It is the act of invoking, understanding, and expressing an ever greater measure of wisdom, love, joy, courage, tolerance, and charity through our self-expression—both as an individual and as a society. The masterworks of art, science, and commerce can accomplish this invocation and expression of spirit every bit as well as religious organizations—if not far better.

When the Hierarchy does work with religion, It works equally through all of the major religions—not just a chosen one. The Hierarchy represents and promotes the universality of the One Life in which we live and move and have our being. It strives to awaken us to a fuller realization of the inclusiveness of divine love. It understands and operates in harmony with the absoluteness and pervasiveness of divine law and order. Any religious denomination that responds to these wavelengths of the life of spirit will attract the attention of the Hierarchy, and be used by it. Unfortunately, most standard religious groups fail to sound the keynote of these activities. They bury themselves in preserving tradition, performing and promoting simple pieties, to the point where they become the walking dead themselves. All the Hierarchy can do in such instances is wait for these religions to resurrect a true spirit of goodwill.

The Hierarchy is not concerned with promoting any specific dogma, nor in supporting the favored few. It is inclusive, not separative! It is therefore interested in all people, all races, all nations, and all institutions of society expressing more of the true spiritual qualities and charitableness which are the hallmarks of enlightened people and groups everywhere. For this reason, the Hierarchy works in every way It can to oppose and reform injustice, selfishness, bigotry, prejudice, ignorance, and sectarianism wherever it is found, no matter how well disguised or rationalized these attitudes have become in the traditions of certain groups.

The problems of humanity are not just religious or political or scientific. Hatred, bigotry, greed, and stupidity are found in every segment of society. Fear, despair, and isolation are not just problems of mental health; they are issues that cripple every dimension of society, from art to education and government. It is therefore natural to expect to find the invisible hand of the Hierarchy busily engaged in combatting these problems in every part of humanity's experience. But the work of the Hierarchy would not end if it managed to overthrow all of these elements of human immaturity. Indeed, it would just be beginning, since the real work of the Hierarchy is to infuse human life with the creative power of love, wisdom, and will. It is for this reason that the Hierarchy is active in every facet of human civilization, from the arts and science to commerce and health. The light of new love and greater understanding is needed everywhere, and so the work of the Hierarchy takes It everywhere.

This just makes sense. It is a lot easier to teach people the meaning of fair play in the context of business and commerce than as an abstract religious or philosophical concept. It is much easier to help humanity overcome superstition by training people to observe life scientifically than it is by developing more dogma and cant. It is simpler to inspire cooperation and responsibility among people and nations through the avenue of business than through government.

It is unfortunate that our common model for the servant of God is a fanatical evangelist or missionary who harangues the ignorant and pleads with them to repent and reform. When people first hear of the Hierarchy, it is all too easy for them to impose this misfigured caricature of the servant of God on his or her image of Its representatives. Nothing could be further from the truth. True agents of the Hierarchy generally work behind the scenes, inspiring new ideas and movements and reforms in the minds and hearts of those key people who are in a position to make intelligent changes. The methodology of the Hierarchy is to inspire, to lift up, to encourage, and to nurture good potential everywhere. Except in times of unusual crisis, coercion has no role in their effort. Despots and bullies work through intimidation; demagogues stir up fear; and fanatics insist on imposing their cherished solutions to every problem at hand. The Hierarchy, by contrast, seeks to act like a benevolent parent who knows that his children need guidance, love, encouragement, and protection. But these needs cannot be forced on them; they must be taught how to become strong, optimistic, loving, and wise themselves. So they work gently, quietly in the background, encouraging humanity to take the next step forward in maturity.

The Hierarchy is not in the business of condemning or punishing wrong doing or vilifying sinners. It is interested in helping humanity climb out of the muck, not just making us feel guilty for being there. While agents of the Hierarchy may stand up and sound a warning about dangerous trends, they cannot forcibly stop people who are commited to acting with either gross stupidity or prejudice. Just so, they cannot use threats of force or guilt to motivate people to do good things. Being in the business of promoting spirit on earth, they are focused entirely in appealing to the highest and noblest elements within humanity and its institutions. They therefore shun all techniques of manipulation and seduction, no matter how effective they might prove to be—in the short run. They will not incur the certainty of long term disaster for short term gain.

In this regard, the agents of the Hierarchy work with humanity very much as though it were the Prodigal Son, overlooking the mistakes of the past so that the rich potential of the present can still be tapped. These agents have learned, from their own spiritual growth, that humanity will have plenty of opportunities to make amends for the errors it is commiting. Instead of dwelling on them, they seek to give humanity a portion of wisdom or love that can help it now, as well as in the future. So they work through the forces of goodwill, by stimulating the innate impulse to grow and the still small voice of wisdom and conscience within the key people involved. They evoke the sense of responsibility of these people—their capacity to respond appropriately to new elements of spirit and add them to the work they do. In this way, these key players in education, business, government, and other institutions are inspired to internalize new elements of enlightened thought and purpose into their own activities and character. To the degree that this quiet evocation is successful, whole institutions of society can be reformed and new traditions and directions can be established.

A major part of the work of the Hierarchy is to help structure events so that they become valuable teaching lessons for humanity—an obvious example of what to do or not to do. Great planning may go into exposing a scandal in government or the press, for example, not so much to bring down the guilty as to highlight the double standards that have been accepted for years—or the arrogance with which public servants sometimes view the public at large. Similar problems may be orchestrated in order to unmask the hidden agenda of certain social activists, or to underscore the dishonest motives of some educational authorities. At the other end of the spectrum, these carefully-staged events may also serve to promote the work of good people who have faithfully advocated discipline and cooperation in our school system, or a community crackdown on the sale of drugs to their kids. The Hierarchy is just as adroit at using a few shining examples of achievement and excellence to inspire humanity as it is in using a few corrupt examples to warn us to wake up.

It is not necessary for agents of the Hierarchy to convene physically in order to pursue their work. Nor do they communicate with each other by telephone, fax, or even the Internet. They have their own special network for communicating—a network of spiritual telepathy. Ideas are transmitted to members of the Hierarchy telepathically, as are specific requests for assistance. This is a much higher form of telepathy than the usual psychic transference of feeling and impression; it is the impression of spiritual ideas on the wavelength of goodwill. By this means, the scattered family of Hierarchical agents is impressed with noble ideas and creative solutions to humanity's problems and needs. Indeed, this spiritual telepathy is always the mechanism by which esoteric groups are formed and kept together, even in the absence of physical contact.

This process of guiding the major institutions of humanity through skilled agents may seem cumbersome to those who believe simplistically that guidance from the World Teacher or Christ comes as direct lightning bolts of wisdom. If such communication were possible (without electrocuting the agent receiving the message), human civilization would have achieved perfection long, long ago—but without any of us developing the maturity and skills to sustain such perfection.

How are the agents of the Hierarchy recruited? It is not just enough to be in a position of power or influence; after all, many highly selfish and even unskilled people end up in posts of influence or authority. Agents of the Hierarchy are chosen by the amount of love, wisdom, and strength that they invest in the pursuit of their daily goals. When a certain measure of skill is blended with a specific level of spiritual maturity, the resulting light that is radiated by the individual becomes a link that draws him or her to the attention of the Hierarchy. Of course, many agents volunteer to work for the Hierarchy before they incarnate; once they receive their education and develop a mature personality, they begin their chosen work. Others prove their usefulness by the quality of life they live and the suitability of their achievements.

There is a tremendous range among such agents. Some are clearly saintly in character and can be recognized as such during their physical lifetimes. A few of these agents are given the great honor and challenge of embodying some divine force in their character and lifestyle. Examples of this kind of agent would be Albert Schweitzer and Mother Teresa, both of whom exemplified aspects of divine compassion. Their lifestyles demonstrated this quality; as a result, the examples they set became part of the very message they came to earth to deliver. Like Schweitzer, these people may also write and say many worthwhile things, but their beingness and character speak most clearly and loudly. As a result, the message they bring us is especially magnetic, enduring, and healing.

Other agents of the Hierarchy are not so overtly saintly, but they are just as important to the work of enlightening humanity. They will be innovators in their chosen field, be it science, the arts, education, business, government, or the healing profession. Since they are embodying aspects of creative wisdom rather than love, and do not perform conspicuous acts of charity among the downtrodden, they are not usually recognized as saints. Nonetheless, they make powerful and irreplaceable contributions to humanity and society through the new inventions, methodologies, or insights that they deliver.

Many of these agents labor in the field of science, where they are responsible for the marvelous technological breakthroughs which so profoundly affect humanity. A single innovation such as the automobile, the telephone, or television can have a universal impact on humanity, changing forever the way we live our lives. Beyond this, it is undoubtedly true that more has been done in recent generations to relieve the suffering of people by advances in medicine, public health, agriculture, animal husbandry, and education than by all of the religious workers put together! Problems such as starvation, disease, epidemics, and superstition have been far more effectively alleviated by scientific and technological solutions than by social protests or the prayers of the devout. For this reason, many agents of the Hierarchy devote themselves to the work of bringing through technological innovations which enrich and heal the misery of human life.

The appearance of Sigmund Freud and Carl Jung during the infancy of the science of psychology was no accident. Through these twin geniuses and their disciples, the Hierarchy was able to nurture and guide the development of this new branch of human understanding. Other outstanding examples of Hierarchical agents who transformed the life of civilization would be Nikola Tesla, in the field of electricity; Luther Burbank, toiling in the field of horticulture; and Joseph Lister, who revolutionized the practice of medicine.

Sometimes the innovation occurs in the realm of government. The Founding Fathers of the United States are a brilliant example of the Hierarchy at work. It was no fluke that the key people who were needed to shape this nation at its birth were all alive at the same time and place. It is not even especially extraordinary, for it is commonplace for the Hierarchy to invest this kind of planning and cooperation in any project it deems especially vital. As a result, a new nation was created that invested its power in the citizens of the country itself—not in a king or a dictator or an oligarchy. The resulting system of government broke new ground as an example for other nations throughout the world. Moreover, the guarantees of freedom that were enunciated in the Constitution and its Bill of Rights became a beacon for expressing this specific spiritual quality in a way that had never been possible before.

Later on, at the time of the worst crisis this nation has ever faced, Abraham Lincoln was able to make an extraordinary demonstration of cooperation, inclusiveness, and charitableness. Not only did he perform invaluable service for his country by preserving its union, but he simultaneously embodied an example of charity and inclusiveness which has never been surpassed, and probably never even equalled. He remains a hero and model for all times—someone whose qualities we can all aspire to and seek to emulate. He set a tone for governing which still manages to inspire us—in our better moments—over a century later. As such, he is an outstanding example of how agents of the Hierarchy not only help us convert crisis into opportunity, but also set brilliant examples for others to follow. Such a person becomes, for a few generations at least, a visible symbol of the conscience of the group they serve.

Innovation and inspiration for society often comes through agents in the creative arts. Writers such as George Orwell, Charles Dickens, Victor Hugo, and H.L. Mencken are just a few examples of those who have used the written word to awaken humanity to the problems besetting them—and some of the possibilities for resolving them. Dickens focused attention on the deplorable conditions for children and debtors in Victorian England. Victor Hugo played a similar role in France, and also pointed out the hypocrisy of the clergy and the gross materialism of the church at that time. Orwell alerted a more modern generation to the corrupt agenda of Marxism in particular and excessive government in general, as well as the misleading emotional appeal of false utopias. And even though Mencken has unjustly fallen from grace due to the political correctness of certain groups with axes to grind, he was a clarion voice for many years encouraging Americans to think clearly and sanely about the cultural issues of life.

The subtle influence of the Hierarchy can also be seen in the contributions of Thomas Edison, Henry Ford, and the Wright brothers at the turn of the century. Those who would scorn technological breakthroughs as trivial compared to philosophical or theological innovations need to reflect upon the fact that the light bulb has extended the hours each day by which we can read, the automobile and other forms of transportation have effectively shrunk the size of the world, and industry in general has given us the leisure time and the resources to pursue greater activities in education, the fine arts, and much more.

Sometimes the message of the Hierarchy is so subtle that it must be demonstrated by example for others to see. Occasionally, the message is so new and revolutionary that it can only be presented through the creative arts. The fine arts and music are especially powerful in the presentation of these more subtle messages. Examples of this kind of Hierarchical message can be found in the poetry of Walt Whitman, the paintings of Thomas Cole, and the music of J.S. Bach.

The initial spokespeople for these messages are often forced to work in obscurity, because the general public is not yet responsive to their inspiration. Nevertheless, they plant a seed that can flourish and reform the thinking of large groups, in due time. All social institutions are influenced by such agents—people who point out the need for reform and innovation. Their work is often met with a strong measure of resistance from the forces of the status quo, but the power of a great idea, once launched, is unstoppable. It sets in motion forces that cannot be reversed.

In due course, these enlightened ideas begin to flourish—first as a dream for a few, then as an incipient movement, next as a growing trend, and finally as the leading edge of evolutionary change. Examples of this kind of progression from an inspired idea to reform and change in society can be seen in the civil rights movement of the 1960's and 1970's, and in the fall of Marxism in the early 1990's in Eastern Europe. Other examples of innovation and the evolution of enlightened ideas can be found in the progressively more humanistic approaches being championed in business and in the delivery of medical services.

Of course, it is one thing to spot, in retrospect, the great giants of enlightenment and innovation in science, medicine, education, government, and philanthropy. It is not nearly so easy to discern the more inconspicuous agents of the Hierarchy who toil in a less visible state of recognition. Many of these people fail to be recognized for their contributions simply because they are too far ahead of their time. As Milton put it, "They also serve who only stand and wait," and while they are waiting, the noble beliefs and values and insights with which they have filled their minds and hearts take root in other minds and hearts—in other people who will take up their banner and continue their crusade. Through their quiet, unheralded efforts, they radiate the light and energies which eventually provide the stimulus and substance for the efforts and reforms of untold numbers of people around—and after—them.

In these ways, the Hierarchy performs its work, nurturing the evolution of humanity's collective character and energizing the spiritualization of civilization.

THE STRUCTURE OF THE HIERARCHY

The idea of a spiritual hierarchy was first introduced in the writings of H.P. Blavatsky and annotated in detail by Alice A. Bailey. Their writings, plus the work of the Theosophical Society, the Arcane School, the School of Esoteric Studies, and others have sketched out most of the significant factual details about the organization of the Hierarchy. Unfortunately, knowledge about the Hierarchy does not necessarily translate into understanding of the Hierarchy, let alone contact with it. In the one hundred years since Blavatsky first introduced the concept of the Hierarchy to the West, a lot of false impressions and sheer nonsense about this group have been generated. The result is a tendency for some people to project or interject elements of their own imagination, fears, or fantasy into their thinking about this subject.

It is not uncommon, as a consequence, to find nearly illiterate people with great expectations who are convinced that they are in direct contact with leaders of the Hierarchy—if not the Christ Himself—and have important work to do. Others are likewise convinced that some great sage from the past is dictating to them the secrets of establishing world peace and personal harmony through the right kind of breathing. Sometimes it is not just an individual but a whole group around him that believes that they are "a direct factory outlet" for the latest orders from the new avatar of the Aquarian Age.

There is no question that some physical people are in contact with the leaders of the Hierarchy—and may even be leaders themselves. But the real ones do not go around announcing themselves to the public. Even in private conversations with other members of the Hierarchy, these links to the inner dimension are seldom mentioned. Indeed, one of the major hallmarks of a true agent of the Hierarchy will be his or her modesty and discretion—in other words, an ability to remain behind the scenes and not demand recognition for the work being done. True agents do not engage in bragging contests about their spiritual knowledge and gifts. This is not to suggest that they are modest to the point of "hiding their light"—that would be a denial of both their humanity and their spirituality, and might well cripple their spiritual duties. But self-aggrandizement, blatant egotism, and the solicitation of admiration from others by hinting at special knowledge, unique gifts, and arcane connections are out of bounds for agents of the Hierarchy.

Like civilization, the major departments of the Hierarchy reflect the diverse interests and creative work of humanity. These major departments are usually called "ashrams," a Hindu word for group. Each ashram oversees one major creative initiative of society. The best known are those ashrams which are responsible for education. The esoteric work of these ashrams is to teach and guide individuals who are ready to tread the spiritual path in the lessons of enlightenment, spiritual telepathy, and discipleship. But agents of these ashrams can also be found promoting the true principles of education at every level throughout the world. The ashrams that worked with Blavatsky, Bishop Leadbeater, Annie Besant, A.P. Sinnett, Alice Bailey, and Rudolph Steiner were primarily of this type.

Other ashrams are just as important, but less well known. They work to supervise the spiritual refinement and advancement of governments, scientific exploration, the creative arts, psychology, medicine, business, and religion. It takes discerning eyes to recognize their invisible influence, however, because the common concept of spirituality held by the average person bears little resemblance to the work of the Hierarchy in infusing new spirit into society. Happiness, niceness, the hope of peace, and freedom from physical needs rank high on the wish list of most people, but they are nowhere to be found on the priority list of concerns of the Hierarchy!

As painful as it may be, it is necessary to cultivate a certain measure of discernment in order to detect the invisible presence of Hierarchical influence or activity in some institutions of society. The Hierarchy is not usually interested in those causes which create great excitement in the press and popular support among the masses; It focuses Its involvement in challenging humanity to grow in skill, awareness, and virtue. And so, even though the Hierarchy is involved in solving the problem of world hunger, It directs Its efforts to inspiring advances in agriculture, promoting self-sufficiency, and encouraging birth control, not in supporting world hunger crusades, benefit rock concerts, or government welfare programs.

It must be understood that many of the world's popular "crusade" causes have been infiltrated by individuals with their own private agenda—an agenda that varies vastly from their public claims. They may profess to be a champion of consumer interests, for example, even though their real goal is to destroy business. They may claim to promote minority rights, but their actual goal may be to exploit differences in race, class, and gender. They may pretend to promote peace, but all of their actions indicate that they are divisive troublemakers. They may claim to protect the environment, but their real goal is to prevent the use of modern technology to advance human civilization. They may declare that they love education, but their primary interest lies in gaining power for themselves, not teaching children or adults.

In many cases, such crusades are diametrically opposed to the work of the Hierarchy; the efforts of these people may actually undo, on a large scale, what the Hierarchy has been trying to demonstrate on a small scale, so that the rest of humanity can learn from it. An important part of appreciating the work and structure of the Hierarchy lies in learning to discriminate between the true work, which is often behind the scenes or even controversial, and the popular efforts of people who are light years away from becoming agents of the fifth kingdom.

In government, for example, the Hierarchy's top priority is to make the governments of the world less of a burden on their citizens and more responsive to real national needs. Our modern governments are huge concentrations of power. The opportunity to abuse this power is enormous—but so is the opportunity to use it to advance humanity and the legitimate needs of the citizens. When officials succumb to temptation, the Hierarchy works behind the scenes to expose their corruption and initiate reforms. When officials show an aptitude for working creatively with their great power, the Hierarchy likewise works to help create a climate in which these ideas and programs can flourish. The Hierarchy does not favor one system of government over another; rather, it strives to cultivate greater honesty, fairness, and effectiveness in every system.

Owing to the incredible power of government to inflict harm on vast groups of people, the Hierarchy also works to encourage governments to redress injustices fairly—*not* through arbitrary legislation that perpetuates the divisions of society. It also strives to promote reconciliation, peacemaking, and compromise as preferred ways of settling conflicts, rather than anger and hostilities. It has been remarkably successful in this endeavor over the years, even though very few people recognize or appreciate Its involvement.

Other ashrams work through the creative arts to kindle new ideas and spark the cultural enrichment and refinement of the masses. The arts can be powerful mechanisms for teaching people new ways of looking at life. As Goethe put it, "A person should hear a little music, read a little poetry, and see a fine picture every day, in order that worldly cares may not obliterate the sense of the beautiful which God has implanted in the human soul." Great art, for example, has the power to teach ordinary people to see life more fully—to absorb not just an image but also its meaning and inner power. Inspired music lifts us up to abstract levels and can promote subtlety and organization in our thinking. Profound literature stimulates the imagination and prompts the mind to detect hidden consequences, new horizons, and inner levels of meaning. All forms of art help us learn to sense the symbolic significance and relevance of what we see and hear. While such refinements in human consciousness may seem unimportant in a world of suffering and tragedy, they in fact provide the key for transcending the impoverished, materialistic elements of society. It is through our capacity to recognize and embrace the subtle elements of life that we can move beyond the material world, entering into the realm of spirit.

Knowing this, the Hierarchy is always involved—behind the scenes—in inspiring receptive artists, writers, musicians, and performers to transport the rest of us to transcendent levels of awareness, where we can entertain new possibilities and ideas. One of the great projects of the Hierarchy in literature in this century has resulted in the brilliant masterworks in the field of science fiction. The books of Robert Heinlein, A.E. van Vogt, Clifford Simak, Colin Wilson, Dave Duncan, and others contain marvelous insights into the nature of the inner life. Often, the works of a few good novelists, composers, and artists can do far more to awaken the presence of spirit in people than a whole stadium filled with ministers, priests, and rabbis. So this is where the Hierarchy expends its efforts.

In science, the work of the Hierarchy is designed to forge new pathways of understanding into the phenomena and laws of life. Of course, it is not the discovery of a longer burning light bulb that matters to the Hierarchy. Its interest lies in revealing the inner laws of life and the reality of the subtle levels of energy and matter. It also trains humanity to cultivate the mental skills needed to operate in a truly scientific way. In medicine, the recent renaissance of interest in the use of homeopathy, acupuncture, radionics, and other forms of energy healing has been inspired by agents of the Hierarchy. This effort, though on a small scale, is slowly pushing medical science to an awareness of the need to work with the subtle energies of the human body in both diagnosis and treatment. It is also gradually promoting the idea that the human system is composed not just of one body but of several—that it is a multidimensional system living in a multidimensional universe. It is necessary to treat a disease like cancer, for instance, in the emotional and etheric bodies, as well as the physical, if medical science hopes to produce a cure, not just remissions. Indeed, the work of the Hierarchy in helping medical science discover its full potential will produce many new discoveries and breakthroughs in the next century that will revolutionize the way we think about our human condition, disease, and healing.

The leadership roles in the Hierarchy are occupied by individuals who have completed the human phase of the spiritual path and have become Adepts or Masters. These Individuals may or may not have a physical body, but They seldom emerge from behind the scenes to play a visible role in the human drama. They embody divine principles and powers. Their knowledge of the higher dimensions of life and their skills are far, far beyond the comprehension of the average educated human being. It would be misleading even to think of them in physical terms, for instance, because they do not interact with the rest of the Hierarchy—or humanity—through physical means. The language they employ is a combination of abstract thought and esoteric symbols, rather than any earthly tongue.

This is not to suggest that agents of the Hierarchy never meet physically or speak physically with one another. Agents are as human as anyone else. But most Hierarchical communication is accomplished by "dropping" a new idea as a hint into the thinking of a responsive scientist, educator, politician, business person, or artist. It is then up to the receptive person to register the idea, appreciate its significance, and do something meaningful with it. Coercion, propaganda, enticement, manipulation, and obfuscation are not part of the style of the Hierarchy. This more subtle approach may seem ineffective, but it is more pure, direct, and powerful in the long run. Because the receptive person is internally inspired, there is far less danger for misdirection and distortion of the basic message than if the guidance were delivered orally. Such intuitive communication can make a direct impression on the brain and memory system and set in motion controlled associations that will lead to correct deductions and conclusions. The message can also be reinforced as often as necessary to produce total comprehension. Furthermore, once the inspired person acts, he or she can then speak with the authority and conviction of a thinker who works with noble ideas at archetypal levels—the level at which Hierarchical guidance occurs.

While it can be helpful to think of the Hierarchy as the true government of humanity, It is not laden down with the bureaucracies we find attached to every physical government. The Hierarchy works on the wavelengths of cooperation and effectiveness. The individuals making key decisions all work at the level of soul consciousness. As a result, there is an absence of the pettiness, egotism, power tripping, deception, and jealousy that so often poison the average bureaucracy. Self-aggrandizement simply is not possible at the level of soul consciousness, which is dominated by the will to serve the highest good of all. Self-aggrandizement is wholly an earthbound concept that cannot exist in a mind that is free of the conditioning force of materialism and its resulting petty values and perspectives. The workers and agents of the Hierarchy are linked together by their dedication to a common purpose. While agents of the Plan characteristically pursue their projects intensely, there is no disagreement among them about basic principles, themes, or even the pace of the ideas and projects the Hierarchy promotes.

In other words, in the Hierarchy enlightened ideas and plans rule the day, not the opinions, fantasies, and wishes of power hungry humans. At this level, religious differences do not exist—because the agents of the Hierarchy deal with the inner essence of spirit, not the outer trappings of belief. National differences are unimportant, because the agents of the Hierarchy are citizens of the world first and citizens of a birth or chosen country second. The objective ideas and plans of the mind of God are the inspiration and the final arbiter for all decisions.

The Hierarchy is a model for what humanity can become, in due time. The senior members of the human race already occupy positions of power and authority in the Hierarchy. They have become part of the Hierarchy because they have demonstrated the ability to work effectively without the burden of competitiveness, prejudice, racism, selfishness, or any form of pettiness and divisiveness. More to the point, they are able to work in direct rapport with spirit. For this reason, they are able to formulate and clearly transmit elements of the divine Plan into works and projects here on earth.

This is the mission of the Hierarchy.

Not everyone who works with the Hierarchy is consciously aware of this connection. Obviously, the leaders and senior members of the ashrams are consciously aware of the role they play, as would be all discarnate agents. But many people who are immersed in the rush of daily activities may be wholly unaware that they are being guided and directed by the Hierarchy, except to wonder occasionally if they are not being inspired by God or the Christ. These are intelligent, creative people who are committed to a life of moral responsibility and enlightened service. They are able to be inspired directly by the soul, even though they may not appreciate this fact.

Direct contact with the soul is always the primary prerequisite for effective cooperation with the Hierarchy. Therefore, anyone who would seek to assist the Plan must first develop a character and motivation that attune him to the life of the soul. He must expand his self-concept to incorporate his divine nature. He must restructure his motives so that they are fueled by goodwill. He must furthermore demonstrate a growing ability to express wisdom, love, strength, and peace in his approach to life. Finally, he must prove the ability to express these spiritual qualities with consistency in daily life.

Unfortunately, large numbers of people who believe they are very advanced on the spiritual path, and presume that they are agents of the Hierarchy, have no direct contact with the soul. In these people, the spiritual life exists far more in their imagination and their desires than in their spiritual talents and a mature self-expression. This demonstrates that the imagination can be a powerful tool for inventing an elaborate relationship with a Master or an ashram. The images created by such people seem real and alive, but they are just thought-forms devoid of any real intelligence or spirit. The sad fact is that such people end up trapped in their own wish life, occupied full time by their dreams and fantasies but unable to go beyond them into the realities of the soul. It becomes a barrier to soul awareness, not an open door.

Other people, lacking knowledge of how the Hierarchy actually works, keep themselves busy fighting the evil they find in the world, convinced that this is their mission to "do good." A few of these fighters are sincere and truly want to do good, but their efforts are crippled by their naïve focus on hating evil. They need to learn to respond to the soul, instead of imperfection or corruption. Many of these crusaders, however, have no real interest in doing good—they are actually promoting the very evil they attack, first by condemning it and then by arousing fear and vulnerability in their followers. They are not guided by the soul.

The first recommendation to anyone who would seek to participate in the work of the Hierarchy, therefore, is to begin by cultivating soul awareness. The would-be agent should embark on an ongoing program to purify the emotions, purging them of fear, anger, doubt, sadness, self-pity, pettiness, and arrogance. He likewise needs to work to enrich the mind—not just by building up knowledge, but far more importantly by developing the active capacities of discrimination, discernment, organization, and intuition. He should make a major effort to review and revise his sense of purpose, major beliefs and values, and priorities, seeking always to integrate more and more of the qualities of the soul into his character and self-expression. Unless the personality is growing toward spiritual maturity, soul consciousness will not be possible.

Sadly, the Western tradition of cultivating soul consciousness in this fashion is not very popular—or even welcome—in many "spiritual" circles. The most common forms of spiritual practice still hinge upon passive devotion and surrender to the higher life, which then allegedly pours into the personality and remakes it without our conscious effort. While this approach to enlightenment may seem plausible, there is a hidden danger in it which is usually not mentioned. Abject devotion of this nature can easily lead the aspirant to focus too much love on the traditions, dogma, and ritual of the religious life, instead of the spiritual realities underlying them. As a result, the careless devotee ends up practicing spiritual *idolatry*, rather than spiritual *contact*—he ends up worshipping, for example, the image and teachings of a saint or guru, rather than making contact with the soul and divine life.

Many people who think of themselves as devout Christians, Moslems, or Hindus fall into this trap. They typically have no inkling that it is their *concept* of God and their religious *traditions* that they worship—not the life of God at all! Such people are often viewed as "good" and even "saintly" by their associates, who would reject any criticism of them as unkind and unspiritual. Yet the fact remains that they are motivated not by spirit but by their personal love of peace, comfort, and security, plus their personal sympathy for the suffering, the lame, and the underprivileged. They love, but without any spiritual vision. They are genuinely kind, but they express this kindness in affirmations, prayers, visualizations, and sweet talk, rather than constructive projects or changes. They want to help, but end up attacking only the symptoms of problems rather than healing the core issues and causes of the problems. They are unfailingly sympathetic, but identify too readily with the suffering of the world to be effective. They lack the detachment and wisdom to initiate true redemptive reforms. In other words, these sweet, devotional types have only traveled part of the way on the spiritual Path. They have learned to hum the music, but not to compose the hymns! They have still not learned how to register the divine forces of wisdom, love, joy, peace, and will *at the abstract level of the soul*, and integrate these forces into their own self-expression and activities. As such, they are still unprepared to work with the Hierarchy in pursuing the divine Plan for the spiritualization of humanity.

It may seem to some that these comments are unfair and unkind to good people who are seeking to know and experience God's love. But the issue at hand is not that of learning to know and experience God's love; it is preparing ourself to work as an agent of the Hierarchy. If we limit ourself to experiencing God's love, we can perpetuate a highly personal, emotional approach to spirit that actually obscures the greater need for the intelligent use of love in service to humanity. The work of the Hierarchy cannot be entrusted to anyone who has not yet replaced his highly personal attitude with the impersonal approach of the soul.

Too many people striving to contact God have confused the experience and expression of divine love with such human traits as flattery, permissiveness, and the unconditional acceptance and indulgence of whatever other people do or say. Nonetheless, there is a huge difference between tolerance and permissiveness, and an even greater gap between divine love and the acceptance of everyone and everything "the way they are."

The rules of the life of spirit are neither arbitrary nor mean-spirited. Neither are they capricious. They are based on the universal laws and principles of the divine Plan. As such, they have been enunciated and shared with us not to intimidate us or make us feel guilty, but to help us fulfill our complete destiny as spiritual beings. We can invent our own way, if we wish, but such a course will merely delay our spiritual progress. Nonetheless, when we are ready to accept the discipline, rules, and sacrifice of the life of spirit, we can get back on course.

The soul-infused person is directed by and dominated by far different standards and motives than the average human being. As the Christ told His disciples, *"Those who love me will keep my commandments."* Loving God with all our heart and mind and soul and might means much more than hugs and kisses for our friends! We must become responsive to the divine Plan as well as divine qualities such as wisdom, truth, and justice. Above all, we must become workers who implement the Plan of God, not just a devotee of the Creator.

Our first real contact with the Hierarchy comes as we take up some endeavor which contributes to the great Plan of the Hierarchy. Usually, this first step is a small one; we defend or support the work of someone who is already laboring as an agent. As we volunteer our support repeatedly in this way, we become responsive to the wavelength of the Hierarchy and its work. The simplicity of this contact may disappoint some who think in grand terms of ceremonies, prayers, and invocations of the Great Ones. But pleading is a waste of time; curiosity and fascination with the Masters is equally irrelevant. On the other hand, if we continually ask ourself: "What can I do for the Hierarchy and Its Plan?" we may find ourself thrust into a situation where we can help.

In other words, it is up to us to begin the work of serving humanity. By becoming active and useful in refining our awareness and spiritualizing the work we do, right where we are in life, we demonstrate commitment, ability, and the capacity to serve.

Our legitimate efforts, no matter how humble, will attract the attention they merit. If we simply wait for a Master or Adept to appear and hand us an assignment, we will wait in vain.

Our own talents and interests provide us with the best clues of what kind of work will be useful. Some people, of course, believe that serving God must involve some act of conspicuous charity to the most hopeless and downtrodden elements of society. Not much of the work of the Hierarchy is done through soup kitchens or leper colonies, however, as useful as they may be. Such activities are helpful in alleviating the pain and hardship of specific individuals, whereas the primary interest of the Hierarchy lies in nurturing the growth of humanity by enriching it with new elements of spirit—for example, by exposing the failure of education to promote excellence, by mending the schisms of society through the cultivation of cooperation and respect, and by prodding the business community to become more sensitive to the needs of employees, customers, and the general public. Its chief focus therefore lies in challenging the institutions of society to better meet the needs of mankind, rather than in serving the needs of individuals.

As a result, virtually any significant activity can become a challenge to demonstrate the life of spirit on earth. Just by adding cheerfulness, integrity, and the quest for excellence to the way we approach our work, we strengthen the presence of spirit on earth. By replacing competitiveness with encouragement of others and support for their efforts, we demonstrate goodwill. By seeing the larger purpose of commerce, science, and the arts, and working to implement this purpose as much as possible, we lift our mundane activities into the light.

A teacher can start working with the Hierarchy, in other words, just by strengthening his or her dedication to and skill in nurturing the best within each student. An artist can start serving the Hierarchy by learning to serve the ideal of beauty more perfectly, while rising above the constant pressures of society to champion the dark side of society, sentimentality, and chaos. An ordinary citizen can start working with the Hierarchy by thinking with clarity about the issues of society, and not just be duped by the loudest, most strident opinions of the day.

As the light of our integrity and commitment begins to shine more brightly, we will probably be drawn into the outer circles of agents who are consciously cooperating with the Hierarchy. Such encounters are opportunities which test our discernment and dedication. Do we respond favorably to the encounter, by getting involved in or supporting the work this agent is doing? Or do we react by criticizing or undermining his or her work? The decision to support the work of legitimate agents of the Hierarchy and withdraw our interest from groups that are working at cross purposes is one of the big tests we must undergo. It is also one of the easiest ways for a spiritual aspirant to make himself or herself useful to the Hierarchy.

Regrettably, the failure to support the work of the Hierarchy when the opportunity is presented is one of the most common sins of omission found on the spiritual path. The work of spiritualizing civilization would proceed far more rapidly, if aspirants could learn to recognize the invisible presence of the Hierarchy in the projects It is involved in throughout society, supporting them as appropriate and defending them as necessary.

As discernment grows, so do our opportunities to serve humanity. Much of the work of the Hierarchy today lies in the field of promoting creativity and the full development of the noble human mind. Toward this end, It is busy encouraging humanity to sharpen its skills of discrimination and discernment, as well as abstract thinking skills to deal with archetypes, the intuition, and the subtle levels of life. The Hierarchy is likewise involved in promoting a more refined picture of spiritual and human maturity. One of the best ways to cultivate spiritual strength, for instance, is to master the intelligent expression of tolerance and patience. As we learn these lessons in our own life, it becomes possible to teach others their value as well. In this way, we contribute to the work of the Hierarchy.

Sometimes, our service is performed just by being a good role model. Words can be ignored and appeals can be scorned, but a shining example still gets through to others, at least at a subconscious level. The example of enlightened living set for us by Jesus speaks even more profoundly than His words. His patience, tolerance, and kindness stood out like a beacon at a time when the heart of religious practice was thought to be the faithful observance of rules and traditions. His ability to summon the power and love of God effortlessly to perform miracles must have struck home forcefully to a people who had been taught to fear a wrathful God.

Even though we cannot reach the stature of Jesus, each of us can set a good example of enlightened speech, mature attitudes, and noble behavior. We can use our role as parent, office worker, salesperson, citizen, or friend to demonstrate the life of spirit in ordinary circumstances. As our skill in doing this grows, so will the arena of our service. The great businessman Andrew Carnegie found it natural to devote the last thirty years of his life to philanthropy, because it was a logical extension of his character and spirituality. Instead of giving handouts to the needy, however, he served humanity as a whole, by funding schools and libraries throughout the world.

Sometimes the expansion of our field of interest gives us a bully pulpit from which we can rally public attention to the need for reform. Dr. C. Everett Koop, the recent surgeon general, found that he could use his position to promote an issue he had advocated throughout his whole career—the value of a healthy lifestyle as an investment in preventing illness and promoting wellness.

In addition to learning to respond to such opportunities to support the work of the Hierarchy, we can also add prayers and invocations on behalf of humanity. This work can be done through the simple act of blessing humanity and its civilization, or by reciting a special prayer, such as *The Great Invocation,* as written by Alice Bailey. The exact structure of the prayer is not important, so long as its intent is to strengthen the connection between heaven and earth and to externalize more of our divine potential through our own character and through civilization.

Whether in prayer or through good works, however, it should be obvious that noble beliefs and good intentions are not enough. The Hierarchy needs agents who are capable of acting in constructive ways, producing enlightened results. It is not enough to have faith that God is at work trying to promote peace and cooperation among all people. We must become the peacemaker in our world. We must become the example of cooperation at the office. We must become the epitome of responsibility as a citizen. We must become a channel for divine progress on earth—not just someone who prays occasionally for a miracle.

In order to work with the Hierarchy in a meaningful way, therefore, it will be necessary to adjust our values, goals, and expectations about human life to match those of the soul. This is not a simple task that can be worked at for a week and then set aside. It is a fundamental reversal of our perspective on life that will require as much as ten to twenty years to complete. We must do nothing less than leave behind our personal, materialistic beliefs and values and replace them with impersonal, spiritual ideals and principles.

This self-transformation cannot be avoided. Many good people try to tackle the problems of the world with the best of intentions, only to become sidetracked quickly by hypercriticism, intolerance, impatience, bigotry, and irritation. It is relatively easy to recognize imperfection in the world; it is a wholly different proposition to understand the appropriate cure for it. It is even rarer to find a person who possesses the tolerance and love to implement the cure.

Some people sabotage the noble work they would perform by spending more time being angry at the problem than in loving the solution. In fact, some crusaders hypocritically speak of the need for love and tolerance, while encouraging their followers to become angry and hateful—to hate those who, in their words, do not love God. Of course, this largely alienates them all from any meaningful service to God.

Other reformers freely employ fear as a motivating force, stressing the "great danger" all around them and the anxiety "we all feel." As such, they sow seeds of paranoia which estrange their followers further from the life of spirit. It is not just demagogues who use fear to promote their dirty little agendas, either; many of the most popular charities in this country regularly use fear to raise funds and promote their purposes. Such tactics are clear advertisements that the work being done by such a group is probably not the work of the Hierarchy.

Those who would work with the Hierarchy must clearly understand that the work of promoting goodwill, truth, and justice *must be performed in that spirit.* Goodwill in thought, intention, and speech is the primary calling card of agents of the Hierarchy. For this reason, leaders who whip up a crowd into a frenzy of fear or anger in order to get their attention are definitely not being overshadowed by the Hierarchy. Their methods are wrong-headed, their efforts are wrongly motivated, and their results are destructive. Such people often have great sympathetic appeal as they lash out against the ills of society, but they rarely offer much "help" beyond the level of arousing indignation and sharing the pain of those who suffer. They end up doing more to encourage despair and alienation among the oppressed than they do to solve any real problems.

Unless we understand the need for self-examination and purification, we are apt to get ourselves into a lot of mischief. There are many more self-promoters "working" on the problems of humanity than there are agents of the Hierarchy. Our own efforts to help humanity may well become derailed if we have the misfortune to tangle with one of these "prophets" of fear and anger. Feigning to be hurt by our opposition to their methods, they will lash out at us for having the gall to criticize their methods or the deficiency of their programs. They will not even hesitate to suggest that it is we who are being unspiritual, *unkind,* as they put on a "hurt little child" expression and play for sympathy.

Hierarchical agents are not judged by their kindness. Kindness can kill just as much as malice. The drug addict would think it a kindness for others to support his or her habit. Arrogant know-it-alls would consider it a kindness for everyone else to subordinate their will and common sense to them. It is therefore necessary to examine where we are brainwashed by conventional thinking, and where we have learned to transcend popular opinion and be inspired by the soul. We must then continue the work of disconnecting from conventional wisdom and strengthening our connection to the perspective of the soul.

As one who loves spiritual truth and divine order, the agent will be compelled to defend them, stand up for them, and promote them as often as possible. The agent of the Hierarchy will often be asked to work against the fads and popular beliefs of the masses. As such, he runs a tremendous risk of being misunderstood by many of the very people who are best suited to help.

In today's society, for example, some of the most popular crusades for reform deal with environmental protection, the transformation of religion into political activism, racial and gender discrimination, and consumerism. The need for corrections does exist in all of these fields, and some of the leaders who have emerged have indeed accomplished something worthwhile—even inspired. But each of these crusades has also spawned opportunistic leaders who are motivated mainly by greed and self-aggrandizement, not Hierarchical purpose. Even though they have captivated the public's imagination, these leaders fail to serve the divine Plan to bring the life of spirit to earth. As a result, they harm "the cause" far more than help.

Our personal values, goals, and opinions are so colored by popular thought that it takes a major re-examination of our attitudes and priorities to begin to see these issues from the perspective of the Hierarchy, not through the dogma and propaganda of charismatic advocates. Indeed, we may be so persuaded by the emotionalism of popular leaders that our first reaction to the truth may be to be offended. How dare anyone try to tell us that animal rights or environmental reforms are not the highest priority of the Hierarchy! But they are not. And if we remain polarized in an emotionally-focused belief that they ought to be, we simply remain a victim of popular faddism. To work in any meaningful way with the Hierarchy, we will have to rise above this trap.

We cannot serve the Plan if we deliberately shock people with guilt.

We cannot serve the Plan if we fill people with fear.

We cannot serve the Plan if we promote ignorant ideas.

We must therefore re-educate ourselves, so that we are able to look at life from the perspective of the soul. In this regard, the first few steps are always the most difficult. Once we learn to view problems from the point of view of the light of the soul, and not the judgments of society, the reversal becomes relatively easy. We also begin to understand that humanity and mass consciousness are being "seeded" with these same enlightened ideas and values. Slowly, they will be understood, at first by the intelligentsia, and then later by the masses.

The very act of service will speed up this reversal of attitude as well. Serving the Plan of God is the most powerful way to invoke the life of spirit—and the most powerful stimulus to personal growth and spiritual maturity. Spiritual service—as opposed to passive adoration of the divine—forces us to make a practical demonstration of our spiritual gifts and resources. It impels us to link our efforts to reform earth with the qualities of the heaven within us. It forces us to strive for the highest possible quality in everything we do.

To this work, we can then add a conscious and deliberate invocation of the life of spirit—and the Hierarchy. Even though invocation alone would never be enough to make contact with the Hierarchy, once we are engaged in serving the Plan the proper use of invocation will greatly strengthen our ability to do the work before us. The work we do as an agent of the Hierarchy is, after all, a shared labor—shared by us and Those who work with us. If we personalize it too much, it ceases to be the work of the Hierarchy and becomes just "our work." By constantly invoking the help and blessing of the Hierarchy that stands behind us, however, we maintain the spirit of shared work. This attitude makes it much easier to radiate the light of spiritual truth and love through us and the work we do. In addition, it helps us ground new life and light of spirit in our life—in our character and in the world around us, not just in our words and deeds.

In this way, we fulfill our portion of the Plan of God—and humanity takes one more step toward fulfilling its work, too.

THE WORK OF HUMANITY

One of the great dangers of the spiritual path is the temptation to succumb to spiritual selfishness. Even though the idea of "spiritual selfishness" is obviously oxymoronic, its practice is all too common. It is not unusual to hear gurus and other "authorities" warn against involvement in things of the earth, on the grounds that it would delay our progress in transcending the earthly plane—if not interfere with the karma of others. These experts further suggest that the effort to help others is just an ego trip—and the ego is meant to be annihilated. The result: a first-rate case of spiritual selfishness.

The work of the spiritual path must include far more than just our personal enlightenment. Recognizing our spiritual birthright and developing our divine potential is unquestionably a major part of the work before us. But it is not enough! If we are truly learning to work with divine love, at some point the force of this inflowing goodwill and charity will begin to broaden our concern for others, our awareness of the human family, and our obligation to serve God. We will also begin to realize that our increasing capacities for tolerance, wisdom, affection, courage, and patience do not mean very much unless we put them to work. The logical way to employ these wonderful skills is by serving the divine Plan.

Even if the personality is slow to discover this truth, the soul already knows it. And it is the soul that directs our spiritual development, not the personality. The soul knows in fullness what the personality knows only vaguely—that no man is an island. The soul is a cell in the body of humanity, a spark within the divine flame. By its very nature, it is committed to participating in the work of spiritualizing the character of the human race and our civilization. It has been committed to this work for millions of years.

The Hierarchy, in other words, does not only represent an opportunity to serve; it is our destiny. It is what we are becoming. It is at the vanguard of everything good and noble that is happening in the grand experiment of the human race. If we want to be in the vanguard as well, we had best learn to participate in the work of the Hierarchy.

For eons, of course, people have believed that God revealed Himself to humanity and worked exclusively through religious leaders, priests, ministers, and rabbis. When we think about divine revelation, we automatically think in terms of temples and churches. We split society into two halves—the ecclesiastical and the secular. The arts, science, education, government, and business may be important elements of civilization, but we regard them as "secular." We do not think of them in terms of the spiritual life.

Some religionists go even further, labeling everything that is outside the realm of religion as "humanistic," as though the human and the divine were mutually exclusive. This type of labeling does serious injury to our thinking. It creates an artificial world in which there are both spiritual and secular activities, but the two must never be brought together. Such arbitrariness is, of course, absurd—as in the doctrine of the separation of church and state. It may be desirable to keep religion out of government and vice versa, but it is disastrous to try to keep the life of spirit out of our political life. It cannot be done, no matter how much petty minds clamor for it.

We need to begin to see humanity as an important player in the divine drama, with civilization as one of its great accomplishments. We are not finished with the work of civilization, of course, but we have progressed far enough to know that it is a grand project. We have also progressed far enough to appreciate that every facet of civilization, not just religion, is potentially an expression of divine life.

In fact, most of the major institutions of civilization are presently far more responsive to the life of spirit and creatively innovative than any of the major religions, which are so busy preserving the dead letter of the past they have not grown or evolved in any significant way in hundreds of years.

In **government,** the work of humanity, as inspired by the Hierarchy, is to establish societies in which the individual responsibility and personal freedom of every citizen can flourish. The spiritual work of government is obviously much more subtle than preserving law and order and providing education, roads, and other services. Throughout history, governments have served the role of drawing groups of people together and cohering them into a much larger group, spawning a common culture, traditions, and identity. This work continues today on a much larger scale than ever before, as nations struggle to sort out and harmonize the myriad divisive voices within their borders that clamor for special rights and unique privileges. Through these struggles, the nations of the world are preparing humanity to recognize its essential unity—its esoteric existence as the body of Christ.

Each nation has its own special role to play in the work of spiritualizing civilization. In England, the task is to evolve and demonstrate the benevolent use of power—in particular, the democratic use of power for the good of its citizens. In Germany, the esoteric work of government is to cultivate harmony and healing in the midst of crises and conflicts. The job of the United States is twofold: to instill the value of freedom throughout the world by example, and synthesize one cohesive nation out of many people and many cultures. It may at times seem as though these nations are heading in the wrong directions, but once the wrong direction is detected by the masses of their citizens, corrective measures will be implemented and balance restored. In this way, important lessons are learned.

In **the arts,** the work of humanity, as inspired by the Hierarchy, is to enrich consciousness. The arts have an amazing capacity to stimulate awareness both in groups and in individuals, awakening us to possibilities and realities we might never imagine otherwise. If it were not for the arts, life on earth would be unbearably mechanical, pedestrian, and buried in aging traditions. The creative arts constantly encourage us to become aware of the subtle and symbolic meanings of ordinary events. They teach us mental skills of association and organization that cannot be learned in any other way. The arts demand that we embrace and comprehend complex thought processes such as patterns, gestalts, abstractions, syntheses, harmonies, and resolutions.

The arts lead us out of our material focus and introduce us to the rich inner world of imagination and abstraction. The mastery of creative thought represents a first major step toward full intuitive awareness. The arts also reveal the relationship between the realm of ideas and the problems of daily living. As we pointed out in our earlier series of essays, *The Art of Living,* our own character and lifestyle can and should be approached as a creative work of art that is gradually perfected through daily experiences. The arts help humanity and civilization learn this important lesson.

In **science,** the work of humanity, as inspired by the Hierarchy, is to discover and build with the order and design of the universe—not just the physical universe, but all of the higher dimensions as well. The more refined study of nuclear physics is an exciting frontier of science at present, and will eventually lead to proof of the subtle side of life—even the fact of the human soul as the originating intelligence of the body and personality. Beyond this, science serves to promote the correct and skillful use of the mind as an agent of discovery and innovative work. It is the need for scientific thinking that will lead humanity to perfect the intellectual powers it needs to move beyond its current emotional focus and begin working as a mentally polarized being. While the antediluvian element of humanity continues to squawk about the conflict between reason and faith, science plods onward, seeking new discoveries—and in the process adds knowledge and reason to faith, as scripture admonishes us to do.

In **the healing arts,** the work of humanity, as inspired by the Hierarchy, is not only to continue its work of alleviating human suffering, but also to educate humanity in the nature of health and the basic principles of healing. The spiritual destiny of the healing arts is to reveal the nature of the soul as a healing resource, and to develop methods for harnessing and integrating divine energies of health into our personality. The research that will make these developments possible will lead health professionals into an awareness of the subtle forces and energies which make up our subtle bodies. In due course of time, in fact, the healing arts will become more preoccupied with the study of human consciousness and how it develops than in the symptoms of physical distress. The infant science of psychology is setting the stage for these discoveries.

In **business and commerce,** the work of humanity, as inspired by the Hierarchy, is to break down the barriers of isolation that have divided humanity, promote the internationalization of civilization, and elevate the quality of physical life. Historically, it has always been the traders and the commercial adventurers who set sail for distant lands and established the first contact between nations. It has usually been business and commerce that has initiated most of the great changes in human living conditions as well. It was private industry, for example, that built the railroad that linked the east coast with the west coast in America in the nineteenth century—a feat that was hailed as the greatest engineering feat of that century. It was industry that united the nation in this way, not government or religion or education.

At a more subtle level, the Hierarchy uses commerce as a vehicle to promote a more refined understanding and spiritual use of human and natural resources. This work embraces a broad perspective, but includes a sensible understanding of the nature of wealth and what it takes to create and sustain wealth. Eventually, the spiritual laws that govern the creation and spending of wealth will be fully revealed—and when they are, they will be revealed largely through people in business and commerce. At present, most of human thinking about wealth has been generated by people outside of business—people without wealth. As a result, it is highly colored by their envy, their divisiveness, and their lack of experience. Humanity has been duped into trying such unworkable ideas as welfare, entitlements, and the redistribution of wealth. Through all the experiments, however, business has continued to demonstrate that hard work and initiative produce wealth, that wealth expands human opportunity, and that the only enduring solution to poverty is productivity. Indeed, business has done more in the last one hundred years to feed the hungry and help the needy than any other institution of society.

In **education,** the work of humanity, as inspired by the Hierarchy, is to prepare individuals for mature self-expression, not just in the intellect but also in the whole of the character. The first stage of this work is to prepare children to be thinking, responsible adults. The second stage, which is usually overlooked, is to promote character building and enlightened citizenship. Once upon a time, the whole work of education was under the auspices of religion. But once it succumbed to the temptation to supplant thinking with dogma, religion's effectiveness as an educator broke down. The same situation is arising once again, now that government has taken over the supervision of education. It is attempting to supplant thinking with a political social agenda. It will be necessary to divorce education from government before any real reforms can occur.

One of the spiritual themes of education is to make every student aware of his or her citizenship in the world and his or her roots in a rich culture of ideas. In many respects, the institution of education is the most critical of all to the work of spiritualizing civilization, as it trains the thinking, maturity, and expectations of each generation. We must therefore work hard to restore the virtues of excellence and achievement to our schools, and recognize the bankruptcy of such current trends as "minimal standards."

In **religion,** the work of humanity, as inspired by the Hierarchy, is to make people aware of the nature of spirit and the spiritual design for each of us—and humanity as a whole. It is time for religion to reawaken to its spiritual duties—its obligations to the rest of civilization. It is no longer appropriate for religion to divorce itself from the humanistic pursuits of civilization and culture; it must swallow a dose of humility and self-examination and see how tragically it has failed to keep pace with its role in society. It must repudiate the rules and traditions and dogma which keep it focused in the past, and rekindle its responsibility to serve humanity in the present. Some might argue that churches do this through their charitable and missionary work. But why are churches involved in missionary work when they are failing to live up to their responsibilities at home? Far from instructing their followers in the nature of spirit, most churches today have just become community social centers. Indeed, so much of modern religion—all religions—has become earthbound and materialistic that its true role has been all but forgotten.

What ought modern religion be doing? To begin with, it needs to catch up with the rest of humanity, by bringing its ancient spiritual principles and revelations up to date. It needs to make these ancient principles relevant and useful to a modern world. Secondly, it needs to bring the *presence* of spirit and divine life back into the church and temple, not just words of praise and professions of faith. The original "church" was not a building with a big mortgage; it was a group of people who gathered to worship, pray, and celebrate the gifts of spirit. They came together to find God—and were not afraid to summon angelic forces, divine archetypes, and spiritual blessings in pursuit of that quest. The work of religion is to help people to find and incorporate their divine possibilities. Until it recaptures this vision, modern religion will be sadly out of step with the true work of humanity.

There is much more that can be written about the work of humanity in each of these key institutions of society—government, the arts, science, the healing arts, business, education, and religion. Indeed, the work of spirit through each of these is so powerful and important that we will focus on each of these institutions, one at a time, in our next set of essays—the final volume in this series on *The Life of Spirit.*

Spirit is not something "up there" that has no relevance to this life. It is alive in our mind and heart, and is eager to become more active in our lives. The same is true for humanity as a whole. Spirit is very much involved in our culture and activities. In fact, it is not possible to have any true idea of the scope and power of spirit until we fully appreciate the dynamic and vital role it plays in every facet of human society.

As we begin to grasp this full scope of the life of spirit, our personal world begins to expand to embrace the breadth and depth of our existence as a race of people with one common source and life. In this way, it becomes possible for enlightenment to come to the entire race—not just individual super-achievers. In fact, it has been the design of spirit all along to enlighten society, not just a chosen few here and there. The work of salvation and redemption is targeted toward the human race as a whole, not just lonely aspirants on the Path.

It is therefore a fact, not just a possibility, that we all live and move and have our being within the one divine life shared by all. It is a fact, not just a speculation, that life is multidimensional and universal. It is a fact, not just a hope, that we all have a rich and powerful resource in our soul—and this inner resource links us with a much greater one, the soul of humanity. This, of course, is the Hierarchy.

As we reflect on these larger concepts, it becomes possible to grasp the reality that huge streams of ideas link us with both the past and the future. In addition to the immortality of the soul, there is something immortal that we deal with every day, as we struggle with the challenges of business, government, the arts, or whatever. It is the larger, spiritual dimension that is to be found within these institutions of humanity. This larger dimension gives meaning to our own work, just as our own work, if approached properly, serves the Plan of the Hierarchy.

There is a destined Plan of perfection for humanity; Its guardian is the Hierarchy. But there is only one way it can be implemented on earth, and that is through our own individual wisdom, love, and efforts. Each of us has the opportunity to participate in this work, if we choose to do so. If we do, then we open ourselves to one of the most powerful spiritual forces on earth.

It will transform our life—and the life of humanity, too.

ABOUT THE AUTHORS

In the late 1960's, Dr. Robert R. Leichtman's interest in intuition and spiritual growth caused him to close his medical practice and devote his energies to personal psychic work, lecturing, teaching, and writing. His pioneer work as a psychic consultant to psychiatrists, psychologists, and medical doctors has helped him become recognized as one of the best psychics in America today. Dr. Leichtman is also the developer of "Active Meditation," a comprehensive course in personal growth and meditative techniques. This teaching is aimed at helping people better understand their lives and develop intuitive skills. He is the author of the paperback series, *From Heaven to Earth,* also published by Ariel Press. Dr. Leichtman currently resides in Baltimore, where part of his time is spent continuing the healing work of Olga Worrall at the New Life Clinic.

Carl Japikse grew up in Ohio. A graduate of Dartmouth College, he began his work career as a newspaper reporter and freelance writer. He has worked for several newspapers, including *The Wall Street Journal.* In the early 1970's, he left the field of journalism and began pursuing his current interests: teaching personal and creative growth, lecturing, and consulting with businesses and individuals. Mr. Japikse is the developer of "The Enlightened Management Seminar," an educational program for executives and managers, and the "Enlightened Classroom," a program for teachers, as well as various courses in spiritual growth, and the author of *The Light Within Us, Exploring the Tarot, The Hour Glass,* and *The Tao of Meow.*

Together, Dr. Leichtman and Mr. Japikse are the authors of *The Life of Spirit* and *The Art of Living* essay series, *Active Meditation: The Western Tradition, Forces of the Zodiac, Enlightenment,* and a four-book interpretation of the I Ching: *Healing Lines, Ruling Lines, Connecting Lines,* and *Changing Lines.*

THE LIFE OF SPIRIT

The complete series of 31 essays written by Dr. Robert R. Leichtman and Carl Japikse in *The Life of Spirit:*

The Spiritual Person
The Spiritual Path
Defeating Evil and Sin
The Power of God: The Mother Aspect
The Power of God: The Son Aspect
The Power of God: The Father Aspect
The Treasures of Spirit
Redeeming Life
Psychic Dimensions of the Life of Spirit
The Role Death Plays in Life
The Trials of Initiation
The Path To Transfiguration
Praying Effectively
Enlightened Confession
The Act of Meditation
Invoking Divine Life
Worshipping God
Making Life Sacred
Finding Heaven on Earth
Linking Earth with Heaven
Harnessing Esoteric Traditions
The Inner Teachings of the Bible
Working with Angels
The Work of the Hierarchy
The Divine Workshop of Government
The Divine Workshop of the Arts
The Divine Workshop of Science
The Divine Workshop of the Healing Arts
The Divine Workshop of Business and Commerce
The Divine Workshop of Education
The Divine Workshop of Religion

The full set of five volumes may be ordered for $50 postpaid.

THE ART OF LIVING

Robert R. Leichtman, M.D. and Carl Japikse have also
written a 30-essay series called *The Art of Living:*

Enriching the Personality
The Practice of Detachment
Finding Meaning in Life
Building Right Human Relationships
The Spirit of Generosity
Joy
Living Responsibly
The Nature and Purpose of the Emotions
Cultivating Tolerance and Forgiveness
Seeking Intelligent Guidance
The Bridge of Faith
Discerning Reality
Cooperating with Life
The Mind and Its Uses: Parts I and II
Coping with Stress
Enlightened Self-Discipline
Inspired Humility
The Act of Human Creation: Parts I & II
The Work of Patience
The Pursuit of Integrity
The Way to Health: Parts I and II
The Process of Self-Renewal
Filling Life with Beauty
Becoming Graceful
The Importance of Courage
The Noblest Masterpiece: Parts I and II

The full set of five volumes may be ordered for $45, post-paid. Call 1-800-336-7769 for information about ordering individual volumes from either essay series.

Orders can be placed by toll-free telephone or by sending an order, plus a check for the appropriate amount, to Ariel Press, P.O. Box 1387, Alpharetta, GA 30239.

ACTIVE MEDITATION

Active Meditation is rapidly becoming recognized as *the* most thorough and insightful explanation of meditation in print. Yet it is not just the most complete book ever written on meditation. More importantly, it is a masterful statement of the emerging Western tradition of personal and spiritual growth.

The tone set by authors Robert R. Leichtman, M.D. and Carl Japikse emphasizes the practical nature of meditation. To them, the subjects of meditation and personal growth are inseparable. They decry the passiveness which has crept into so many systems of meditation, presenting instead a strong case that meditation is most effective when it is *active*. Indeed, the active practice of meditation is the Western tradition.

In the book the authors describe:
- What meditation is—and is not.
- How meditation accelerates personal and spiritual growth.
- The nature of the higher self—and its relationship with the personality.
- How to contact the higher self.
- The work of integration.
- The skills of meditation and how to use them.
- Seven techniques of Active Meditation.
- Group meditations.
- Aids to meditation.
- Problems associated with meditating.

Throughout, the constant goal of the authors is to strip away the vagueness and obscurity often associated with meditation. In many ways, *Active Meditation is* the most encyclopedic book ever written on meditation.

"It is refreshing to find a book that offers the reader practical guidelines for establishing contact with his or her own inner authority....It is a definitive statement."—*New Realities.*

Active Meditation sells for $19.95 plus $3 postage.

FORCES OF THE ZODIAC

Forces of the Zodiac sets forth a brilliant new way of using astrological information. Written by Dr. Robert R. Leichtman and Carl Japikse, it is a practical guide to using the psychological and spiritual forces available to us to accelerate personal growth, expand our creativity, enrich relationships, strengthen leadership skills, solve problems, and seize opportunities.

This book is the result of six years of research, which began with the observation that certain trends and qualities influence everyone alike in each monthly sign of the zodiac, regardless of natal sign. This insight resulted in a series of monthly reports prepared intuitively by the authors—something like psychological weather reports predicting the conditions, problems, and opportunities of each sign.

This research set the stage for *Forces of the Zodiac,* a comprehensive treatment of this revolutionary approach to astrology. The book consists of a thorough description of astrological influences, what they mean to us, how to tune into them, and how we can harness them in our life. This description is then followed by twelve chapters, each focusing on one of the twelve signs and exploring:

• The major archetypal forces that characterize the sign.
• The symbolism of the sign.
• How the major forces of the sign influence our lives and challenge us to grow.
• The problems of each sign and how to resolve them.
• The opportunities of the sign and how to seize them.
• How to tune in intuitively to the forces of the sign.

Forces of the Zodiac is meant to be used as a guide book to spiritual living. Both in scope and layout, it is a companion to *Active Meditation* by the same authors.

Holistic Medicine hailed *Forces of the Zodiac* as "top priority reading" for everyone seeking "to use the forces and energies of the moment to heal and grow."

Forces of the Zodiac sells for $19.95 plus $3 postage.

I CHING ON LINE

The I Ching is an ancient Chinese system of philosophy that helps us understand the immutable workings of cosmic law and intelligence. It can also be used to understand specific problems of our personal life and to help us make decisions concerning the right action to take in any situation.

I Ching On Line is an innovative computer program that weds this ancient system with the modern technology of the IBM PC and the Macintosh computers. It makes the I Ching much easier and quicker to use.

- It automatically records your question.
- It randomly generates hexagrams and changing lines.
- It brings up the appropriate commentary in seconds.
- It allows you to enter notes.
- It lets you store and print out each consultation for further reference.
- It lets you access up to four different commentary modules: one on health, one on business and personal decisions, one on relationships, and one on growth. In this way, you can tailor the use of the program to specific needs, question after question.

But this is not just an automated I Ching. The commentaries have been written by Dr. Robert R. Leichtman and Carl Japikse especially for this program.

The healing commentary, in other words, has been written specifically for health questions—not only for physical health but psychological health as well. The same is true for the other modules, too, resulting in a tool that can be used with precision and clarity.

The basic program and four modules of I *Ching On Line* are available for $100.00. This package includes the program and module diskettes, a copy of the full text of all four books, and complete instructions.

Please specify which version of the program—IBM or Macintosh—you are ordering. Place orders with Ariel Press, P.O. Box 1387, Alpharetta, GA 30239. Or call toll free 1-800-336-7769.

The text of the four modules comprising I Ching On Line is also available as four individual books:

Healing Lines, the text of the healing module.

Ruling Lines, the text of the decision making module (business and personal).

Connecting Lines, the text of the module on relationships.

Changing Lines, the text of the module on personal and spiritual growth.

While the set of four books is included with the computer program at no extra charge, the four books are also available without the computer program. The I Ching can be consulted through these books in the old-fashioned way, either with three coins or with yarrow sticks.

These books are fresh, modern restatements of the I Ching by authors Robert R. Leichtman, M.D. and Carl Japikse. They strip away the obscurity of the I Ching while retaining its full power as a tool of practical philosophy.

The cost of each book is $7.95 plus $2 shipping. The cost of the set of four books (without the computer program) is $30, plus $4 shipping.

These books can be ordered directly from the publisher, Ariel Press, at P.O. Box 1387, Alpharetta, GA 30239. Or call toll free 1-800-336-7769.

ENLIGHTENMENT

Dr. Robert R. Leichtman and Carl Japikse have been writing a series of lessons in spiritual growth for a number of years. Called *Enlightenment*, the lessons deal with the general theme of learning to become an agent of light. More specifically, the lessons fall into 7 categories:

• The Light of Learning, in which the authors present their philosophy of education and what it means to grow.

• The Lights of Heaven, an exploration of the archetypal forces of the mind of God and how each of us can learn to tap and harness these forces for change in our lives.

• The Revelation of Light, in which Dr. Leichtman and Mr. Japikse outline the nature of the psychic dimensions of life and what it means to work at these levels.

• Embodying the Light, a guide to enlightened self- expression and how it can enrich our lives.

• Embracing the Light, in which the process and techniques of spiritual integration are described.

• The Light Which Penetrates, in which the authors examine the use of the human mind to make sense of the world around us and to nourish itself on the wonderful advances of human civilization.

• Our Companions in the Light, which expands our awareness of other forms of life on earth and how a reverence for the beauty and glory of all life enriches our own.

Each lesson discusses one aspect of one of these themes of living, then presents an easy-to-apply exercise describing how to put these new ideas to work in our own life.

A new lesson is produced every two months and is sent to subscribers by first-class mail as they are ready.

In addition, 24 of the lessons have already been written.

Lessons 25 through 30 are being produced during 1997 and will be sent to subscribers as they are ready.

The cost of subscribing to lessons 1-30 is $60. Additional years will be available at $15 a year. To order, call Ariel Press at 1-800-336-7769 and charge the order to any major credit card.

Ariel Press also publishes a set of six books called *From Heauen to Earth*. Each book contains four interviews beween Dr. Robert R. Leichtman and the spirits of prominent psychics, geniuses, and world leaders. They may be purchased individually for $12.95 apiece (plus $2 shipping) or as a complete set for $55, postpaid. The six books in the set are:

The Psychic Perspective–Edgar Cayce, Eileen Garrett, Arthur Ford, and Stewart White.

The Inner Side of Life–C.W. Leadbeater, H.P. Blavatsky, Cheiro, and Carl Jung and Sigmund Freud.

The Hidden Side of Science–Nikola Tesla, Luther Burbank, Sir Oliver Lodge, and Albert Einstein.

The Priests of God–Albert Schweitzer, Paramahansa Yogananda, Andrew Carnegie, and Sir Winston Churchill.

The Dynamics of Creativity–William Shakespeare, Mark Twain, Rembrandt, and Richard Wagner.

The Destiny of America–Thomas Jefferson, Benjamin Franklin, Abraham Lincoln, and a joint interview with seven key spirits from American history–Alexander Hamilton, Franklin, Jefferson, the two Roosevelts, Harry Truman, and George Washington.

Orders can be placed by sending a check for the proper amount to Ariel Press, P.O. Box 1387, Alpharetta, GA 30239. Make checks payable to Ariel Press. Foreign checks should be payable in U.S. funds. In Georgia, please add 6% sales tax.

It is also possible to order by calling toll free 1-800-336-7769 between 9 a.m. and 6 p.m. Monday through Friday and between 1 and 5 p.m. Saturday, charging the order to VISA, MasterCard, Discover, Diners Club, or American Express.

There are many people who are sincerely devoted to growing spiritually and becoming more attuned to their higher selves, yet do not seem to make much progress. They try this method and that technique, but exhaust themselves in a series of false starts. They have enough devotion. They have enough faith. What they lack is *understanding*–a knowledge of how to tread the spiritual path.

The Light Within Us provides this special knowledge. It is a step-by-step guide to spiritual growth which is written to help aspirants of all backgrounds understand what spirit is, what it means to grow spiritually, and how to do it. Written by Carl Japikse, it is a lucid and easy-to-grasp presentation of the timeless knowledge.

The instructions which form the core of the text are a modern, updated translation of an ancient text of raja yoga written thousands of years ago by a teacher named Patanjali. The commentary on each instruction is Japikse's penetrating insight into the demands and requirements of spiritual growth in our twentieth century world.

There are four parts to the commentary:

Part I, a description of the nature of consciousness and the role it plays in understanding the human drama.

Part II, an examination of the spiritual work of integration and how to pursue it.

Part III, an exploration of the responsibilities of creative mastery and the skills of the initiate.

Part IV, a revelation of the light within us and its relation to the light of the world.

Much of the power in *The Light Within Us* is the author's determination to show the practical applications of these principles in our daily life. This is truly a book that helps everyone on the spiritual path.

The Light Within Us sells for $10.95 plus $3 postage. Order from Ariel Press, P.O. Box 1387, Alpharetta, GA 30239. Or call toll free 1-800-336-7769.

THE WORK OF LIGHT

The Life of Spirit is issued by Ariel Press, the publishing house of Light, a nonprofit, charitable foundation.

The purpose of Light is to stimulate the growth of the mind and the creativity of people throughout the world. It was founded by Dr. Robert R. Leichtman and Carl Japikse, two authorities on human consciousness, personal growth, and the creative process. The work of Light is to enrich the human capacity to use the mind and spirit wisely and productively.

The activities of Light include the publications of Ariel Press, a series of taped lectures, the development of new classes, the Books of Light book club, and the presentation of lectures and forums.

Contributing receive a newsletter, "The Work of Light," and all of the mailings of Books of Light.

The cost of a contributing membership is $35 a year for an individual, $50 a year for a family. There are also four other levels of contributing membership: the *fellow,* who contributes $100 a year; the *benefactor,* who contributes $250 a year; the *angel,* who contributes $1,000 a year, and the *founder,* who pledges to give at least $2,000 a year for three years. Fellows, benefactors, angels, and founders receive all of the benefits of the contributing membership. A brochure describing the work of Light will be sent on request.

To become a contributing member of Light, send a check and letter of application to Light, P.O. Box 1387, Alpharetta, GA 30239.

All contributions to the work of Light are fully tax-deductible.